Who the F*ck Told You It Would Be Easy

Life's Challenges Head-On

GALERON PRESS

GALERON CONSULTING

Copyright © 2023 by GALERON CONSULTING

All rights reserved.

No portion of this book may be reproduced in any form without written permission from the publisher or author, except as permitted by U.S. copyright law.

Contents

Preface	VI
Introduction	VII
Prologue	VIII
Preface	IX
Introduction	X
Dedication	XI
1. Chapter 1: Embracing the Struggle	1
The Myth of Overnight Success	2
The Importance of Resilience	7
Learning from Adversity	12
Transforming Challenges into Opportunities	17
2. Chapter 2: Developing a Winning Mindset	22
The Power of Positive Thinking	23
Cultivating Mental Toughness	28
Embracing Self-Reflection	33
Overcoming Limiting Beliefs	38

3. Chapter 3: The Roadmap to Your Goals	43
Setting SMART Goals	44
Crafting a Personal Vision Statement	49
Prioritizing and Time Management	54
Tracking Progress and Adjusting Your Plan	59
4. Chapter 4: The Power of Consistent Action	64
Creating a Daily Routine	65
Overcoming Procrastination	71
Maintaining Motivation	76
Celebrating Small Wins	80
5. Chapter 5: Building a Support Network	84
Surrounding Yourself with Positive Influences	85
Seeking Mentorship and Guidance	90
Establishing a Personal Board of Advisors	95
The Importance of Giving Back	100
6. Chapter 6: Mastering Communication and Influence	105
Active Listening and Empathy	106
Persuasive Storytelling	110
Assertiveness and Confidence	115
Building Trust and Rapport	120
7. Chapter 7: Embracing Change and Uncertainty	125
Developing Adaptability	126
Cultivating an Innovation Mindset	131
Navigating Difficult Transitions	136

Staying Grounded in the Present Moment	141
8. Chapter 8: Personal Branding and Visibility	146
Crafting Your Personal Brand Story	147
Building an Online Presence	152
Networking and Relationship Building	158
Embracing Public Speaking and Thought Leadership	163
9. Chapter 9: Achieving Work-Life Balance	168
Defining Your Personal Values	169
Setting Boundaries and Managing Stress	174
Nurturing Relationships and Personal Growth	178
The Importance of Self-Care and Mindfulness	183
10. Chapter 10: The Path to Lasting Success	188
Embracing Lifelong Learning	189
The Power of Persistence and Patience	193
Celebrating Success and Staying Humble	198
Passing the Torch: Inspiring the Next Generation	203
Epilogue	207
Epigraph	208
Acknowledgements	209
About the Author	210

Preface

In this book, we are going to delve into the realities of life and success, discussing the challenges and obstacles that we all face. Drawing on my experience as a Life Coach, Motivational Speaker, and Experienced Consultant, I will share practical insights and advice to help you navigate your own journey. Remember, no one said it would be easy, but with determination, perseverance, and the right mindset, you can overcome anything.

Introduction

Welcome to "Who the F*ck Told You It Would Be Easy?" This book isn't meant to coddle or comfort. It's meant to be a wake-up call, a brutal reality check, and an absolute game-changer for those willing to listen, learn, and take action.

Prologue

A chilly wind swept through the busy streets of Manhattan. In a small cafe, two entrepreneurs locked in a deep conversation - one a burgeoning success, the other teetering on the brink of failure. As their coffees grew cold, the successful one leaned back, looked at the desperate face across from him, and asked, "Who the f*ck told you it would be easy?"

Preface

This book was born from that single question. It's a journey, a raw and uncensored exploration of what it really takes to succeed, whether in business or life. This is a collection of real stories, gritty insights, and hard-earned wisdom. It's a roadmap through the challenges, the failures, the heartaches, and ultimately, the triumphs.

Introduction

Welcome to "Who the F*ck Told You It Would Be Easy?" This book isn't meant to coddle or comfort. It's meant to be a wake-up call, a brutal reality check, and an absolute game-changer for those willing to listen, learn, and take action.

For the dreamers, the doers, and the unrelenting. This is for you.

Chapter One

Chapter 1: Embracing the Struggle

The Myth of Overnight Success

In today's world, we often hear stories of people achieving instant fame and success, seemingly out of nowhere. These tales can be inspiring but can also create a false impression that success comes quickly and easily. The reality is that success is often a long, hard-fought journey, and the so-called "overnight successes" are the exception rather than the rule. In this section, we will debunk the myth of overnight success and provide you with tools, insights, and real-life examples to help you appreciate the value of hard work and perseverance.

The Hidden Years: The Untold Stories of Struggle

What many people don't realize is that most overnight successes have spent years, if not decades, working tirelessly behind the scenes. Before they were known to the public, they faced numerous setbacks, failures, and heartbreaks. It's essential to acknowledge these unseen struggles and understand that success is not handed to anyone on a silver platter.

For example, Oprah Winfrey, one of the most influential media moguls, had a challenging start in life. Born into poverty and facing abuse throughout her childhood, she overcame countless obstacles to become a successful television personality and entrepreneur. But her journey was far from easy, and her success was the result of decades of hard work, resilience, and determination.

Similarly, J.K. Rowling, the famous author of the Harry Potter series, was a single mother struggling to make ends meet before she found success as a writer. She faced numerous rejections from publishers before her first book was finally accepted, and even then, she continued to face challenges throughout her career. Rowling's success was not handed to her; it was earned through blood, sweat, and tears.

The Formula for Success: Hard Work, Perseverance, and Dedication

The key ingredients for achieving success are hard work, perseverance, and dedication. While talent and luck can play a role, it is your willingness to put in the time and effort that will ultimately determine your success. Here are some essential strategies to help you on your journey:

Set realistic expectations: Understand that success does not happen overnight, and give yourself permission to take the time you need to develop your skills and achieve your goals. Embrace the journey and the process, rather than focusing solely on the end result.

Embrace failure as a learning opportunity: Everyone faces setbacks and failures, but successful people use these experiences to learn, grow, and become better at what they do. When you encounter failure, resist the urge to dwell on the negative and instead focus on the valuable lessons it can teach you.

Develop a growth mindset: A growth mindset is the belief that you can improve and develop your abilities through dedication and hard work. By adopting this mindset, you'll be more motivated to push through challenges and persist in your efforts, ultimately leading to greater success.

Cultivate resilience: Resilience is the ability to bounce back from adversity and keep moving forward despite setbacks. By developing resilience, you'll be better equipped to navigate the inevitable obstacles and setbacks that come with the pursuit of success.

Stay committed to your goals: As you work towards your dreams, it's crucial to stay committed to your goals, even when the going gets tough. Keep your eyes on the prize and remind yourself of why you're doing what you're doing.

Practical Tools for Success: Techniques to Stay on Track

To help you on your journey to success, here are some practical tools and techniques that you can use to stay motivated, focused, and resilient:

Break your goals down into smaller, manageable tasks: This will help you maintain momentum and make progress without feeling overwhelmed. As you complete each task, celebrate your accomplishments and use them as motivation to keep pushing forward.

Develop a daily routine: Establishing a consistent daily routine will help you build positive habits and increase your productivity. Set aside time each day for tasks that move you closer to your goals, and stick to your schedule as much as possible.

Surround yourself with positive influences: The people around you can have a significant impact on your mindset and motivation. Build a support network of like-minded individuals who share your aspirations and can offer encouragement, advice, and support when needed.

Practice self-compassion: Be kind to yourself and acknowledge that setbacks and failures are a normal part of the journey. Treat yourself with the same compassion you would offer to a friend or loved one in a similar situation.

Reflect on your progress regularly: Regularly assess your progress toward your goals, and take note of the lessons you've learned along the way. Use these insights to adjust your strategies and approach as needed.

Real-Life Examples: Stories of Struggle and Triumph

To further illustrate the importance of embracing the struggle and debunk the myth of overnight success, let's explore a few more real-life examples:

Walt Disney: Before creating the iconic Disney empire, Walt Disney faced numerous setbacks and failures. His first animation company went bankrupt, and he was fired from a newspaper job for "lacking creativity." Despite these challenges, Disney persisted in his passion for animation and eventually achieved unparalleled success in the entertainment industry.

Colonel Sanders: The founder of Kentucky Fried Chicken, Colonel Harland Sanders, didn't achieve success until later in life. His restaurant failed multiple times, and he was rejected by over 1,000 potential franchisees before finding a successful business partner. His persistence and dedication to his vision eventually led to the global success of KFC.

Steve Jobs: The late co-founder of Apple Inc., Steve Jobs, was fired from the company he started in his early 30s. This setback forced him to reassess his approach and ultimately led to the development of NeXT, which would later be acquired by Apple. Jobs returned to Apple and led the company to become one of the most successful technology companies in the world.

These examples demonstrate that even the most successful individuals have faced struggles and setbacks along their journeys. By embracing the struggle and maintaining a steadfast commitment to their goals, they were able to achieve extraordinary success.

Conclusion: The Path to Success is Paved with Struggle

The myth of overnight success is a dangerous illusion that can lead to unrealistic expectations and disappointment. In reality, the road to success is often long, challenging, and full of obstacles. By embracing the struggle and maintaining a persistent, dedicated approach, you can achieve your goals and create a fulfilling, successful life.

Suggested Reading and Resources:

"Mindset: The New Psychology of Success" by Carol S. Dweck – This book delves into the importance of developing a growth mindset to achieve success.

"Grit: The Power of Passion and Perseverance" by Angela Duckworth – This book explores the crucial role of grit and resilience in achieving long-term success.

"The Obstacle Is the Way: The Timeless Art of Turning Trials into Triumph" by Ryan Holiday – This book provides insights and strategies for overcoming obstacles and embracing adversity on your journey to success.

Remember, the journey to success is not an easy one, but with the right mindset, dedication, and perseverance, you can overcome any obstacle and achieve your dreams.

The Importance of Resilience

Resilience is the ability to withstand adversity and recover from setbacks, emerging stronger and more determined than before. In the journey toward success, it is inevitable that you will encounter challenges, failures, and disappointments. The ability to bounce back from these hardships is a crucial skill that separates those who ultimately succeed from those who give up. In this section, we will explore the importance of resilience, share real-life examples of resilient individuals, and provide actionable steps and resources to help you cultivate resilience in your own life.

The Role of Resilience in Success

Success is not a linear path, and you will undoubtedly face obstacles and setbacks along the way. Resilience is the fuel that keeps you going, even when the going gets tough. It enables you to adapt to change, learn from your mistakes, and persevere through challenges. Some key benefits of resilience include:

Improved problem-solving skills: Resilient individuals can think critically and creatively to find solutions to challenges, turning obstacles into opportunities for growth.

Enhanced emotional intelligence: Resilience helps you to better understand and manage your emotions, as well as empathize with others. This emotional intelligence can enhance your relationships, both personally and professionally.

Increased self-confidence: As you overcome challenges and grow from your experiences, your self-confidence will naturally increase. This newfound confidence will help you tackle future obstacles with greater ease and determination.

Long-term success: By developing resilience, you are more likely to achieve long-term success. It equips you with the skills and mindset needed to navigate setbacks and pursue your goals relentlessly.

Real-Life Examples: Stories of Resilient Individuals

To illustrate the power of resilience, let's examine the stories of several individuals who faced significant challenges but refused to give up:

Thomas Edison: One of the most famous inventors in history, Edison experienced numerous setbacks and failures throughout his career. Despite these challenges, he persisted in his work, eventually leading to groundbreaking inventions such as the light bulb and the phonograph. Edison once said, "I have not failed. I've just found 10,000 ways that won't work."

Malala Yousafzai: The youngest Nobel Peace Prize laureate, Malala Yousafzai, is a prime example of resilience. After being shot by the Taliban for advocating for girls' education, she not only survived but continued her activism, becoming an international symbol of courage and determination.

Bethany Hamilton: After losing her arm in a shark attack at the age of 13, professional surfer Bethany Hamilton could have easily given up her dreams. However, she demonstrated remarkable resilience and determination by returning to the sport and becoming an inspiration to people worldwide.

Cultivating Resilience: Practical Tips and Strategies

To develop resilience in your own life, consider the following tips and strategies:

Embrace a growth mindset: As mentioned in the previous section, a growth mindset is the belief that you can improve and develop your abilities through hard work and dedication. This mindset is crucial for cultivating resilience, as it encourages you to view setbacks as opportunities for growth and learning.

Practice self-compassion: When you face setbacks and disappointments, it's essential to treat yourself with kindness and understanding. Acknowledge your emotions, and remember that it's okay to feel upset or frustrated. However, don't dwell on these feelings – instead, use them as motivation to keep moving forward.

Build a support network: Surround yourself with positive, supportive individuals who can offer encouragement, advice, and a listening ear during difficult times. Having a strong support system can help you navigate challenges and maintain your resilience.

Set realistic goals and expectations: Be honest with yourself about your abilities and the time it takes to achieve your goals. By setting realistic expectations, you'll be better prepared to handle setbacks and adjust your plans as needed.

Learn from your experiences: When faced with challenges, take the time to reflect on the situation and identify what you can learn from it. Use this newfound knowledge to strengthen your resolve and improve your strategies moving forward.

Focus on what you can control: In any situation, there will be factors outside of your control. Rather than becoming overwhelmed by these external factors, focus on what you can control – your attitude, your actions, and your response to the situation.

Develop healthy coping mechanisms: When faced with adversity, it's essential to have healthy ways of coping with stress and negative emotions. This can include activities such as exercise, meditation, journaling, or talking to a trusted friend or family member.

Practice gratitude: Focusing on the positive aspects of your life can help you maintain a resilient mindset. Regularly practice gratitude by acknowledging the good things in your life, no matter how small they may seem.

Exercises and Techniques for Building Resilience

To further strengthen your resilience, consider incorporating the following exercises and techniques into your daily routine:

Visualization: Visualization is a powerful tool that can help you mentally rehearse overcoming challenges and setbacks. Spend a few minutes each day visualizing yourself successfully navigating difficult situations and emerging stronger as a result.

Mindfulness meditation: Practicing mindfulness meditation can help you develop greater self-awareness and emotional regulation, which are essential components of resilience. Set aside time each day for mindfulness practice, focusing on your breath and observing your thoughts and feelings without judgment.

Journaling: Writing about your experiences, emotions, and thoughts can be a helpful way to process and learn from challenges. Regular journaling can help you gain insight into your resilience and areas for growth.

Affirmations: Positive affirmations can help you maintain a resilient mindset by reinforcing your belief in your abilities and strengths.

Create a list of affirmations that resonate with you, and recite them daily to boost your self-confidence and resilience.

Conclusion: Resilience as the Key to Overcoming Struggles

Resilience is a critical component of success, enabling you to adapt to change, learn from setbacks, and persevere in the face of adversity. By embracing a growth mindset, practicing self-compassion, and building a strong support network, you can cultivate resilience in your own life.

Suggested Reading and Resources:

"Option B: Facing Adversity, Building Resilience, and Finding Joy" by Sheryl Sandberg and Adam Grant – This book offers insights and practical advice on building resilience and navigating life's challenges.

"Resilience: The Science of Mastering Life's Greatest Challenges" by Steven M. Southwick and Dennis S. Charney – This book explores the science behind resilience and offers strategies for developing this essential skill.

"The Resilience Workbook: Essential Skills to Recover from Stress, Trauma, and Adversity" by Glenn R. Schiraldi – This workbook provides practical exercises and techniques to help you build resilience and overcome challenges.

Remember, the path to success is filled with struggles, but by developing resilience, you can navigate these obstacles and achieve your dreams.

Learning from Adversity

Adversity is an inescapable aspect of life, but it is also an opportunity for growth and development. When we face challenges and setbacks, we have the chance to learn from our experiences, build resilience, and emerge stronger and wiser. In this section, we will explore how to harness adversity as a catalyst for personal growth, providing practical strategies, exercises, and resources to help you turn setbacks into stepping stones on your path to success.

The Power of Embracing Adversity

When faced with adversity, it's natural to feel overwhelmed or defeated. However, these challenges can also be viewed as valuable learning experiences. Embracing adversity can lead to numerous benefits, including:

Developing resilience: As previously discussed, resilience is a crucial skill for long-term success. By learning to navigate adversity, you can cultivate this ability to bounce back from setbacks and remain focused on your goals.

Gaining self-awareness: Adversity often reveals our strengths and weaknesses, providing insights into our character and abilities. This self-awareness can be invaluable in guiding our personal and professional growth.

Building problem-solving skills: Overcoming challenges requires creative thinking and resourcefulness. By confronting adversity, you can develop and refine your problem-solving abilities, which can be applied to various aspects of your life.

Expanding your comfort zone: Facing adversity often requires stepping out of your comfort zone and taking risks. By doing so, you can become more comfortable with uncertainty and open yourself up to new experiences and opportunities.

Real-Life Examples: Overcoming Adversity and Learning from Setbacks

Many successful individuals have faced significant adversity, using these experiences as opportunities for growth and development. Consider the following examples:

J.K. Rowling: The author of the Harry Potter series experienced numerous setbacks before finding success. Rowling was a struggling single mother, and her manuscript was rejected by multiple publishers. However, she persisted and ultimately created one of the most successful book series in history.

Oprah Winfrey: Oprah faced numerous challenges in her early life, including poverty, abuse, and prejudice. Despite these hardships, she went on to create a media empire and become one of the most influential women in the world.

Steve Jobs: The co-founder of Apple was fired from the company he helped create, which he later described as a "devastating" experience. However, Jobs used this setback to reassess his priorities, ultimately returning to Apple and leading the company to unprecedented success.

Strategies for Learning from Adversity

To harness adversity as a catalyst for growth, consider the following strategies:

Adopt a growth mindset: A growth mindset, as mentioned earlier, is the belief that you can improve your abilities through dedication and hard work. By embracing this mindset, you can view setbacks as opportunities to learn and develop your skills.

Reflect on your experiences: Take the time to analyze your setbacks and identify what you can learn from them. Ask yourself questions such as, "What could I have done differently?" or "How can I use this experience to improve in the future?"

Seek feedback: Others can provide valuable insights into your strengths and areas for improvement. Seek feedback from trusted friends, family members, or colleagues to gain a fresh perspective on your experiences and learn from your setbacks.

Focus on the process, not just the outcome: When facing adversity, it's essential to recognize that the journey is just as important as the destination. By focusing on the process and the lessons learned along the way, you can transform setbacks into opportunities for growth.

Embrace failure as a learning opportunity: Failure is an inevitable part of life, but it doesn't have to define you. Instead, view failure as a chance to learn, grow, and improve. By adopting this mindset, you can turn negative experiences into positive growth opportunities.

Practice patience and persistence: Overcoming adversity often requires time, effort, and dedication. Stay committed to your goals, and be patient with yourself as you navigate setbacks and challenges.

Cultivate a support network: Surround yourself with people who believe in you and support your growth. A strong support network can provide encouragement, advice, and assistance when you're facing adversity.

Tools and Exercises for Learning from Adversity

In addition to the strategies mentioned above, the following tools and exercises can help you learn from adversity and build resilience:

Journaling: Writing about your setbacks and challenges can provide valuable insights into your experiences and help you process your emotions. Regularly journal about your struggles and the lessons learned to gain a deeper understanding of your growth journey.

Mindfulness meditation: Mindfulness meditation can help you develop greater self-awareness and emotional regulation, enabling you to respond more effectively to adversity. Practice mindfulness meditation regularly to cultivate these essential skills.Develop a personal mantra: Create a personal mantra or affirmation that reminds you of your ability to overcome challenges and learn from adversity. Repeat this mantra to yourself when faced with setbacks to maintain a positive mindset.

Analyze your setbacks: When you encounter a setback, take the time to analyze the situation objectively. Identify the factors that contributed to the challenge and determine what you can learn from the experience.

Setbacks as stepping stones exercise: Reflect on a past setback and consider how it has contributed to your growth. Write down the lessons learned and the positive outcomes that have resulted from this experience.

Conclusion: Harnessing Adversity for Personal Growth

Learning from adversity is a crucial aspect of personal development and success. By embracing setbacks as opportunities for growth, you can develop resilience, expand your comfort zone, and enhance your problem-solving skills. With the right mindset, strategies, and support, you can transform adversity into a powerful catalyst for growth and achievement.

Suggested Reading and Resources:

"Failing Forward: Turning Mistakes into Stepping Stones for Success" by John C. Maxwell – This book offers practical advice on learning from failure and using setbacks as opportunities for growth.

"Rising Strong: How the Ability to Reset Transforms the Way We Live, Love, Parent, and Lead" by Brené Brown – In this book, Brené Brown explores the process of overcoming adversity and the importance of vulnerability in personal growth.

"Adversity Quotient: Turning Obstacles into Opportunities" by Paul G. Stoltz – This book introduces the concept of Adversity Quotient (AQ) and provides strategies for improving your ability to overcome challenges and setbacks.

Remember, adversity is an inevitable part of life, but it's also an opportunity to learn, grow, and become a stronger, more resilient individual. Embrace the struggle, learn from your setbacks, and use these experiences as stepping stones on your path to success.

Remember, adversity is an inevitable part of life, but it's also an opportunity to learn, grow, and become a stronger, more resilient individual. Embrace the struggle, learn from your setbacks, and use these experiences as stepping stones on your path to success.

Transforming Challenges into Opportunities

In the face of adversity, it's easy to feel overwhelmed or defeated. However, by changing your perspective and viewing challenges as opportunities, you can unlock incredible growth and development. This section will explore the importance of shifting your mindset, offering practical strategies and resources for transforming challenges into opportunities for personal and professional growth.

The Mindset Shift: From Obstacles to Opportunities

The way we perceive challenges and setbacks can significantly impact our ability to overcome them. By shifting your mindset from viewing challenges as obstacles to seeing them as opportunities, you can:

Foster a growth mindset: As mentioned earlier, a growth mindset is the belief that your abilities can be developed through hard work and dedication. By viewing challenges as opportunities for growth, you can cultivate this mindset and enhance your personal and professional development.

Increase motivation: When you view challenges as opportunities, you're more likely to approach them with enthusiasm and determination, increasing your motivation to overcome them and achieve your goals.

Enhance problem-solving skills: Challenges often require innovative thinking and resourcefulness. By viewing them as opportunities, you can hone your problem-solving skills and apply these abilities to various aspects of your life.

Develop resilience: As discussed in previous sections, resilience is a crucial skill for long-term success. By learning to embrace challenges and view them as opportunities, you can build this ability to bounce back from setbacks and remain focused on your goals.

Real-Life Examples: Turning Challenges into Opportunities

Many successful individuals have faced significant challenges and turned them into opportunities for growth and development. Consider the following examples:

Richard Branson: The founder of the Virgin Group is well-known for his ability to turn setbacks into opportunities. After his airline, Virgin Atlantic, faced numerous challenges, Branson used these experiences to improve the company and ultimately achieve success.

Sara Blakely: The founder of Spanx faced many obstacles in her quest to create a successful shapewear company, including multiple rejections from manufacturers. However, Blakely persisted, turning these challenges into opportunities to refine her product and eventually build a billion-dollar business.

Walt Disney: The creator of the Disney empire faced numerous setbacks, including bankruptcy and the loss of his first animation studio. However, Disney viewed these challenges as opportunities to learn and grow, ultimately creating one of the world's most successful entertainment companies.

Strategies for Transforming Challenges into Opportunities

To harness the power of perspective and turn challenges into opportunities, consider the following strategies:

Reframe your thinking: Instead of viewing challenges as insurmountable obstacles, try to see them as opportunities for growth and development. This mindset shift can help you approach difficulties with a more positive and proactive attitude.

Break challenges down into smaller tasks: Large challenges can often feel overwhelming. By breaking them down into smaller, more manageable tasks, you can tackle each step with confidence and a sense of accomplishment.

Focus on what you can control: In the face of adversity, it's essential to focus on the aspects of the situation that you can influence or control. This can help you maintain a sense of agency and empower you to take action.

Surround yourself with positive influences: The people you surround yourself with can significantly impact your mindset and attitude towards challenges. Seek out individuals who inspire and motivate you, and who can offer valuable support and guidance when facing adversity.

Continually learn and adapt: Embrace a lifelong learning mentality, and be open to adapting your approach in the face of challenges. By being flexible and open to change, you can more effectively navigate setbacks and turn them into opportunities for growth.

Tools and Exercises for Transforming Challenges into Opportunities

In addition to the strategies mentioned above, the following tools and exercises can help you transform challenges into opportunities and build resilience:

Visualization: Use visualization techniques to imagine yourself successfully overcoming challenges and achieving your goals. This mental exercise can help you build confidence and maintain a positive outlook in the face of adversity.

Gratitude practice: Regularly expressing gratitude for your accomplishments and the positive aspects of your life can help you maintain a more optimistic mindset and increase your resilience when facing challenges.

Reflective journaling: Keeping a journal where you record your thoughts, feelings, and experiences related to challenges can help you identify patterns and insights that can be used to inform your approach to future obstacles.

Seek feedback: Actively seek feedback from others, both in your personal and professional life, to gain new perspectives on your challenges and learn from their experiences and insights.

SWOT analysis: Conduct a SWOT analysis (Strengths, Weaknesses, Opportunities, Threats) when facing a challenge to identify the areas in which you can improve and the opportunities available to you.

Conclusion: Embracing Challenges as Opportunities for Growth

Transforming challenges into opportunities is an essential skill for personal and professional success. By adopting a growth mindset, surrounding yourself with positive influences, and using the tools and strategies provided in this section, you can develop the resilience and adaptability needed to overcome adversity and achieve your goals.

Suggested Reading and Resources:

"The Obstacle Is the Way: The Timeless Art of Turning Trials into Triumph" by Ryan Holiday – This book offers valuable insights on using obstacles as opportunities for growth, drawing on ancient Stoic philosophy and real-life examples.

"Mindset: The New Psychology of Success" by Carol S. Dweck – This book introduces the concept of growth mindset and provides practical strategies for cultivating this mindset to enhance personal and professional development.

"Grit: The Power of Passion and Perseverance" by Angela Duckworth – In this book, psychologist Angela Duckworth explores the importance of grit, or perseverance and passion for long-term goals, in achieving success and overcoming challenges.

Remember, the way you perceive and approach challenges can significantly impact your ability to overcome them and achieve your goals. By embracing the struggle and viewing obstacles as opportunities for growth, you can unlock your full potential and become a more resilient, adaptable, and successful individual.

Chapter Two

Chapter 2: Developing a Winning Mindset

The Power of Positive Thinking

Positive thinking is a powerful tool that can significantly impact your life, leading to increased success, happiness, and overall well-being. By adopting a positive mindset, you can overcome challenges, achieve your goals, and maintain a more optimistic outlook on life. In this section, we'll explore the concept of positive thinking, its benefits, and how you can incorporate it into your daily life.

The Science Behind Positive Thinking

Numerous studies have demonstrated the psychological and physiological benefits of positive thinking. Researchers have found that optimistic individuals experience lower rates of depression and anxiety, better physical health, and longer lifespans. Furthermore, positive thinking can enhance problem-solving abilities, increase motivation, and improve overall performance in various aspects of life.

Some of the key benefits of positive thinking include:

Improved mental health: Positive thinking can help reduce stress, anxiety, and depression by promoting a more balanced and optimistic perspective on life.

Enhanced immune system: Research has shown that individuals with positive attitudes are more likely to have stronger immune systems, which can help prevent illness and promote overall health.

Better coping skills: Adopting a positive mindset can help you better manage stress and adversity, allowing you to navigate challenging situations with greater resilience and mental fortitude.

Increased motivation: A positive outlook can provide the necessary motivation to persevere through setbacks and work towards your goals.

Greater success: Studies have shown that positive thinking is associated with increased success in various aspects of life, including career, relationships, and personal growth.

To harness the power of positive thinking, it's essential to develop specific strategies and techniques to cultivate a more optimistic outlook on life. Below, we'll discuss some practical tips for fostering a positive mindset.

Strategies for Developing a Positive Mindset

Practice gratitude: Regularly expressing gratitude for the positive aspects of your life can help shift your focus from negative thoughts to positive ones. Consider keeping a gratitude journal, where you write down things you're thankful for each day.

Reframe negative thoughts: When you find yourself dwelling on negative thoughts, practice reframing them in a more positive light. For example, instead of saying, "I'll never be able to do this," try saying, "I may not be able to do this now, but with practice and dedication, I can improve."

Surround yourself with positivity: Your environment can significantly impact your mindset. Surround yourself with positive influences, including people, books, and media, to help reinforce your positive outlook.

Engage in positive self-talk: Practice speaking kindly to yourself, focusing on your strengths and accomplishments, rather than dwelling on your perceived flaws or failures.

Visualize success: Spend time each day visualizing yourself achieving your goals and experiencing the positive emotions associated with success. This mental rehearsal can help boost your confidence and motivation.

Set realistic goals: Establishing achievable goals and breaking them down into smaller, manageable steps can help you maintain a positive outlook and stay motivated as you work towards your objectives.

Practice mindfulness: Mindfulness techniques, such as meditation and deep breathing exercises, can help you become more aware of your thoughts and emotions, allowing you to cultivate a more positive mindset.

Suggested Reading and Resources

To further explore the power of positive thinking and learn additional strategies for cultivating a winning mindset, consider the following books and resources:

"The Power of Positive Thinking" by Norman Vincent Peale – This classic book explores the impact of positive thinking on personal and professional success, offering practical techniques for developing a more optimistic outlook.

"The Happiness Advantage: The Seven Principles of Positive Psychology That Fuel Success and Performance at Work" by Shawn Achor – In this book, the author presents seven principles derived from positive psychology research that can help you maximize your potential and achieve greater success in work and life.

"Learned Optimism: How to Change Your Mind and Your Life" by Martin E. P. Seligman – In this groundbreaking book, the founder of positive psychology provides a comprehensive guide to developing optimism and resilience, leading to increased happiness and success.

"Mindset: The New Psychology of Success" by Carol S. Dweck – This influential book explores the power of mindset and how adopting a growth mindset can lead to improved performance, motivation, and success in various aspects of life.

"The 7 Habits of Highly Effective People" by Stephen R. Covey – This classic self-help book provides a framework for personal and professional success, emphasizing the importance of a proactive and positive mindset.

Additional Techniques and Exercises

To help you further develop a positive mindset and mental toughness, consider incorporating the following exercises into your daily routine:

Affirmations: Repeating positive affirmations can help reinforce optimistic beliefs and counteract negative self-talk. Create a list of empowering statements that reflect your goals, values, and strengths, and repeat them to yourself regularly.

Journaling: Writing about your thoughts and emotions can help you gain greater self-awareness and identify patterns of negative thinking. Consider setting aside time each day to reflect on your experiences and emotions, focusing on the positive aspects of your life.

Mindful breathing: Practicing deep, mindful breathing can help reduce stress and anxiety, promoting a more positive and relaxed state of mind. Set aside a few minutes each day to focus on your breath, inhaling deeply and exhaling slowly.

Exercise: Engaging in regular physical activity can help release endorphins, leading to improved mood and mental well-being. Incorporate exercise into your daily routine to support a more positive mindset.

Connect with others: Building strong social connections can help improve your mood and overall mental health. Reach out to friends, family, and colleagues to share your experiences, seek support, and foster positive relationships.

Remember, the journey to developing a winning mindset requires patience, persistence, and practice. By incorporating these strategies and techniques into your daily life, you'll be well on your way to embracing a more positive, resilient, and successful outlook. And as you continue to cultivate mental toughness and harness the power of positive thinking, you'll discover that no challenge is insurmountable, and every obstacle is an opportunity for growth and self-improvement.

Cultivating Mental Toughness

Mental toughness is an essential quality that helps us navigate through difficult times and maintain the motivation to achieve our goals. It is the ability to face challenges head-on, persevere in the face of adversity, and bounce back stronger than before. In this section, we'll discuss strategies and techniques to cultivate mental toughness, helping you build a winning mindset that will propel you towards success.

Overcoming Limiting Beliefs

Limiting beliefs are those negative thoughts and assumptions that hold us back from reaching our full potential. They can take many forms, such as fears, doubts, and self-critical thoughts. To cultivate mental toughness, it's essential to identify and challenge these beliefs, replacing them with empowering thoughts that support our growth and success. Here are some steps to overcome limiting beliefs:

Identify your limiting beliefs: Take time to reflect on the negative thoughts and assumptions that might be holding you back. Ask yourself what beliefs are preventing you from pursuing your goals and dreams.

Analyze the origin: Consider where these beliefs come from, such as past experiences, societal expectations, or negative influences in your life. Understanding the root cause can help you recognize that these beliefs are not based on reality and can be changed.

Challenge and reframe: Question the validity of your limiting beliefs and consider alternative perspectives that support your growth and success. Replace negative thoughts with empowering affirmations that reinforce your strengths and abilities.

Repeat and reinforce: Regularly practice challenging and reframing your limiting beliefs to build mental toughness and create new, positive thought patterns.

Developing Discipline and Consistency

Discipline and consistency are key factors in building mental toughness. They help you establish good habits, maintain focus, and persevere in the face of setbacks. Here are some strategies to develop discipline and consistency:

Set clear goals: Having well-defined, achievable goals provides direction and motivation, making it easier to maintain discipline and stay consistent in your efforts.

Break down tasks: Breaking tasks into smaller, manageable steps can make it easier to stay disciplined and consistent. This approach also provides regular opportunities for success and reinforcement.

Create routines: Establishing daily routines can help you build discipline and consistency by making your desired behaviors automatic and more manageable.

Monitor progress: Regularly tracking your progress and reflecting on your achievements can help you stay motivated and disciplined.

Establish accountability: Sharing your goals and progress with others can provide external motivation and help you maintain discipline and consistency.

Coping with Stress and Pressure

Stress and pressure are unavoidable in our lives, but how we handle them can greatly impact our mental toughness. Here are some techniques to cope with stress and pressure more effectively:

Develop a stress management plan: Identify the primary sources of stress in your life and develop strategies to manage them. This might include setting boundaries, delegating tasks, or practicing relaxation techniques.

Cultivate a support network: Having a strong support network of friends, family, and mentors can help you navigate stressful situations and provide valuable perspective and guidance.

Prioritize self-care: Ensuring that you're taking care of your physical, mental, and emotional well-being is essential for managing stress and maintaining mental toughness. This might include regular exercise, proper nutrition, and sufficient sleep.

Practice mindfulness: Mindfulness practices, such as meditation and deep breathing, can help you stay present and focused, reducing the impact of stress and pressure on your mental well-being.

Learn from setbacks: Embrace failures and setbacks as learning opportunities, using them to improve your skills, knowledge, and resilience.

Embracing a Growth Mindset

A growth mindset is the belief that our abilities, intelligence, and skills can be developed and improved through dedication, effort, and learning. Cultivating a growth mindset is crucial for developing mental toughness, as it encourages us to embrace challenges, persevere through setbacks, and continually strive for self-improvement. Here are some strategies to foster a growth mindset:

Embrace challenges: View challenges as opportunities for growth and development, rather than threats or obstacles to be avoided. This mindset can help you stay motivated and focused on your goals, even when faced with difficulties.

Focus on effort and progress: Recognize that effort and persistence are the keys to success, rather than innate talent or abilities. By focusing on your progress and celebrating small victories, you can build your mental toughness and maintain motivation.

Cultivate a love of learning: Develop a passion for learning and self-improvement, continually seeking out new knowledge, skills, and experiences. This mindset can help you stay curious, engaged, and committed to your personal and professional growth.

Practice resilience: Learn to bounce back from setbacks and failures, using them as opportunities to learn, grow, and improve. This can help you develop the mental toughness required to navigate life's inevitable challenges and setbacks.

Seek feedback and learn from criticism: Embrace constructive feedback and criticism as valuable tools for growth and improvement. By actively seeking out feedback and learning from it, you can build your mental toughness and continually refine your skills and abilities.

Suggested Reading and Resources

To further develop your mental toughness and cultivate a winning mindset, consider exploring the following books and resources:

"Mindset: The New Psychology of Success" by Carol S. Dweck – This groundbreaking book explores the power of the growth mindset and provides practical strategies for fostering it in your own life.

"The Obstacle is the Way: The Timeless Art of Turning Trials into Triumph" by Ryan Holiday – This book draws on the principles of

Stoic philosophy to teach readers how to turn challenges and obstacles into opportunities for growth and success.

"Grit: The Power of Passion and Perseverance" by Angela Duckworth – In this book, psychologist Angela Duckworth explores the concept of grit and its importance in achieving long-term success.

"The Art of Mental Training: A Guide to Performance Excellence" by D.C. Gonzalez – This book provides practical techniques and strategies for developing mental toughness and achieving peak performance.

"The 5 Second Rule: Transform Your Life, Work, and Confidence with Everyday Courage" by Mel Robbins – This book offers a simple yet powerful tool for overcoming fear, self-doubt, and procrastination, helping you build mental toughness and achieve your goals.

By implementing the strategies and techniques discussed in this section, you can cultivate mental toughness and develop a winning mindset that will enable you to face challenges head-on, persevere through adversity, and ultimately achieve your goals and dreams.

Embracing Self-Reflection

In the journey of personal and professional growth, embracing self-reflection is a critical component of developing a winning mindset. As an experienced life coach, consultant, and motivational speaker, I've seen firsthand how the power of self-reflection can transform individuals and propel them toward success. In this section, we'll explore the importance of self-reflection, the practical steps you can take to cultivate this habit, and the resources available to support you on this journey.

The Significance of Self-Reflection

Self-reflection is the practice of regularly examining your thoughts, feelings, and actions to gain a deeper understanding of yourself, your values, and your goals. It's a powerful tool for personal growth, as it enables you to identify areas of improvement, celebrate successes, and make informed decisions about your future. By engaging in self-reflection, you'll be better equipped to:

Identify and address self-limiting beliefs: Uncovering the beliefs that may be holding you back allows you to challenge them and replace them with more empowering and productive beliefs.

Recognize patterns and habits: By reflecting on your past experiences, you can identify patterns in your behavior that may be contributing to your successes or setbacks.

Develop self-awareness: Gaining a deeper understanding of your values, strengths, and weaknesses will help you make more informed choices and align your actions with your goals.

Set realistic goals: Self-reflection can help you evaluate your progress and set achievable goals that align with your values and aspirations.

Enhance decision-making: By reflecting on past experiences, you can learn from your mistakes and successes, improving your ability to make effective decisions in the future.

Foster personal growth: Self-reflection enables you to learn from your experiences, allowing you to evolve and grow as an individual.

Implementing Self-Reflection in Your Life

To reap the benefits of self-reflection, it's essential to incorporate this practice into your daily routine. Here are some practical steps and techniques to help you embrace self-reflection:

Create a dedicated space and time for reflection: Carve out a specific time each day or week to engage in self-reflection. Find a quiet, comfortable space where you can focus on your thoughts and emotions without distractions.

Use journaling as a tool: Writing down your thoughts and feelings can help you organize and process your emotions, making it easier to recognize patterns and gain insights. Consider maintaining a daily or weekly journal to record your experiences, emotions, and observations.

Ask yourself open-ended questions: To encourage deep reflection, ask yourself open-ended questions that prompt introspection and exploration. Examples of such questions include:

What did I learn from my experiences today/this week?

How did I handle challenges or setbacks?

What successes or accomplishments am I proud of?

What areas do I need to improve in?

How can I apply what I've learned to future situations?

Practice mindfulness: Cultivating mindfulness through meditation or other practices can help you develop greater self-awareness and focus on the present moment, allowing you to engage in more effective self-reflection.

Seek feedback from others: Obtaining feedback from trusted friends, family members, or colleagues can provide valuable insights and perspectives that may be difficult to see from your vantage point. Be open to constructive criticism and use it as an opportunity to grow.

Reflect on your values and goals: Regularly assess whether your actions align with your values and long-term goals. This can help you stay focused on your priorities and make adjustments as needed.

Use visualization techniques: Imagining yourself in future situations and considering how you would respond can help you prepare for challenges and develop more effective strategies for handling adversity.

Review and adjust your progress: Periodically review your progress toward your goals and use your reflections to make any necessary adjustments. This will help you stay on track and maintain momentum.

Creating a Culture of Reflection and Growth

As you embrace self-reflection, it's essential to cultivate a mindset that supports personal growth and development. Here are some tips for fostering this mindset:

Approach self-reflection with curiosity: Rather than judging yourself harshly, approach reflection with a sense of curiosity and a willingness to learn from your experiences.

Be patient with yourself: Personal growth is a lifelong journey, and it's essential to be patient with yourself as you navigate the ups and downs of life.

Maintain a growth mindset: Embrace the belief that you can learn, grow, and improve over time. This mindset will help you view challenges as opportunities for growth and remain open to new experiences.

Stay committed to self-improvement: Recognize that personal growth requires consistent effort and dedication. Commit to continually investing in yourself and seeking opportunities to learn and develop.

Cultivate self-compassion: Practice self-compassion by acknowledging your struggles and offering yourself understanding and kindness. This can help you maintain motivation and resilience during difficult times.

Resources for Further Learning

To support you on your journey of self-reflection and personal growth, consider exploring the following resources:

Books:

"The Gifts of Imperfection" by Brené Brown

"The Untethered Soul" by Michael A. Singer

"Man's Search for Meaning" by Viktor E. Frankl

"The Power of Now" by Eckhart Tolle

Podcasts:

The Life Coach School Podcast with Brooke Castillo

The Tony Robbins Podcast

The Best One Yet (BOY) Podcast with Michael Todd

Online courses and workshops:

Greater Good Science Center's "The Science of Happiness" course

Mindfulness-Based Stress Reduction (MBSR) program

The Life Coach School's "Self-Coaching Scholars" program

Apps:

Headspace (meditation and mindfulness)

Reflectly (journaling and self-reflection)

Moodpath (mental health and self-reflection)

In conclusion, embracing self-reflection is a vital aspect of developing a winning mindset. By cultivating the habit of self-reflection and fostering a culture of growth, you'll be better equipped to overcome challenges, learn from your experiences, and achieve your goals. With dedication and perseverance, you can transform your life and unlock your full potential. Remember, the journey of personal growth is a lifelong endeavor, and self-reflection is your trusted companion on this path to success.

Overcoming Limiting Beliefs

Limiting beliefs are thoughts or convictions that hold us back from reaching our full potential. They are often ingrained in our minds from a young age and can result from various sources, such as past experiences, societal expectations, or self-imposed restrictions. Overcoming these limiting beliefs is essential for developing a winning mindset and achieving success. In this section, we will explore practical tools and techniques to help you break free from the constraints of limiting beliefs.

Identifying Your Limiting Beliefs

The first step in overcoming limiting beliefs is to recognize their presence in your life. Here are some tips for identifying your limiting beliefs:

Reflect on your past experiences: Consider the challenges and setbacks you've faced in your life, and explore whether there are any recurring themes or beliefs that have contributed to these situations.

Pay attention to your self-talk: Notice the thoughts and statements you repeatedly tell yourself, particularly when you're facing a challenge or feeling discouraged. These thoughts may reveal limiting beliefs.

Consider your emotions: Strong emotional reactions can often signal the presence of limiting beliefs. If you feel anger, fear, or anxiety in specific situations, take a moment to reflect on the underlying thoughts or beliefs that may be triggering these emotions.

Transforming Limiting Beliefs into Empowering Beliefs

Once you've identified your limiting beliefs, it's time to replace them with empowering beliefs that support your success. Here are some strategies for transforming your limiting beliefs:

Reframe your beliefs: Challenge the validity of your limiting beliefs by reframing them in a more positive and empowering light. For example, instead of thinking, "I'm not good at public speaking," consider the belief, "I can learn to become a confident and effective public speaker."

Gather evidence to support your new beliefs: Look for examples from your own life or the lives of others that demonstrate the truth of your empowering beliefs. This evidence will help reinforce the new beliefs and weaken the influence of your limiting beliefs.

Practice visualization: Visualize yourself embodying your empowering beliefs and achieving your goals. This mental rehearsal can help strengthen your new beliefs and build your confidence in your ability to succeed.

Use affirmations: Develop positive statements that reflect your empowering beliefs, and repeat them regularly. These affirmations can help solidify your new beliefs and counteract the negative self-talk that stems from your limiting beliefs.

Developing a Winning Mindset

With your new empowering beliefs in place, you can begin cultivating a winning mindset that supports your success. Here are some tips for developing a winning mindset:

Set clear and achievable goals: Define specific, measurable, achievable, relevant, and time-bound (SMART) goals that align with your values and aspirations. These goals will provide direction and motivation as you work toward success.

Embrace a growth mindset: Adopt the belief that your abilities and intelligence can be developed over time through effort, persistence, and learning. This mindset will help you view challenges as opportunities for growth and remain open to new experiences.

Cultivate resilience: Develop the ability to bounce back from setbacks and persevere through challenges. Resilience will help you maintain a positive outlook and stay focused on your goals, even in the face of adversity.

Practice self-compassion: Treat yourself with kindness and understanding when you encounter difficulties or make mistakes. Self-compassion can help you maintain your motivation and resilience during challenging times.

Tools and Techniques for Overcoming Limiting Beliefs

Here are some practical tools and techniques to help you overcome your limiting beliefs and develop a winning mindset:

Cognitive Behavioral Therapy (CBT): CBT is a form of psychotherapy that focuses on changing unhelpful thought patterns and behaviors. It can be an effective tool for overcoming limiting beliefs by helping you identify and challenge irrational thoughts, develop alternative perspectives, and implement new behaviors that support your goals.

Journaling: Writing down your thoughts, feelings, and experiences can provide valuable insights into your limiting beliefs and help you track your progress as you work to transform them. Regular journaling can also promote self-reflection, self-awareness, and personal growth.

Meditation and mindfulness: Practicing meditation and mindfulness can help you become more aware of your thoughts and emotions, making it easier to recognize and challenge limiting beliefs. These practices can also promote relaxation, reduce stress, and enhance your overall well-being.

Support groups and coaching: Joining a support group or working with a life coach can provide you with guidance, encouragement, and accountability as you work to overcome your limiting beliefs and develop a winning mindset. Sharing your experiences and learning from others can also offer valuable insights and inspiration.

Real-Life Examples and Case Studies

To illustrate the power of overcoming limiting beliefs, let's explore some real-life examples and case studies:

J.K. Rowling, the author of the Harry Potter series, overcame numerous rejections and personal setbacks before finding success. Her persistence and determination to share her story, despite her initial failures, demonstrate the power of overcoming limiting beliefs about one's abilities and potential.

Oprah Winfrey, a media mogul and philanthropist, overcame a challenging upbringing and numerous setbacks in her career to become one of the most influential and successful women in the world. Her story highlights the importance of resilience, self-belief, and determination in overcoming limiting beliefs and achieving success.

Suggested Reading and Resources

For further learning and exploration on overcoming limiting beliefs and developing a winning mindset, consider the following resources:

"The Power of Now" by Eckhart Tolle – This book offers practical guidance on developing present-moment awareness and overcoming limiting beliefs that hold us back from realizing our full potential.

"Mindset: The New Psychology of Success" by Carol S. Dweck – This influential book introduces the concept of the growth mindset and provides strategies for cultivating this mindset to achieve personal and professional success.

"The Gifts of Imperfection" by Brené Brown – In this book, Brené Brown explores the importance of self-compassion, vulnerability, and authenticity in overcoming limiting beliefs and living a more fulfilling life.

In conclusion, overcoming limiting beliefs is essential for developing a winning mindset and achieving success. By identifying and transforming your limiting beliefs, setting clear goals, embracing a growth mindset, and cultivating resilience and self-compassion, you can create a strong foundation for personal and professional success. Implementing practical tools, techniques, and resources, such as CBT, journaling, meditation, and coaching, can support your journey and help you break free from the constraints of limiting beliefs.

Chapter Three

Chapter 3: The Roadmap to Your Goals

Setting SMART Goals

In this section, we will delve into the art of setting SMART goals to help you create a clear roadmap to achieve your desired outcomes. Setting goals is a critical component of personal and professional success, and SMART goals, in particular, can help ensure your objectives are clear, realistic, and attainable. By understanding and implementing the SMART goal framework, you'll be better equipped to navigate the road to your goals.

The Importance of SMART Goals

SMART goals are designed to provide structure and guidance throughout the goal-setting process. The acronym "SMART" stands for Specific, Measurable, Achievable, Relevant, and Time-bound, which are the essential criteria for setting effective goals. When you set SMART goals, you create a clear path for achieving success by ensuring your objectives are well-defined and within your reach.

The Components of SMART Goals

Specific: A specific goal is one that is clearly defined and easy to understand. To create a specific goal, ask yourself what you want to achieve, why it's important, and how you'll accomplish it. By answering these questions, you'll establish a clear direction and purpose for your goal.

Measurable: Measurable goals allow you to track your progress and determine whether you're on track to achieve your desired outcome. To make a goal measurable, identify the metrics or milestones you'll use to gauge your success. This could be a numerical target, a particular accomplishment, or a specific behavior change.

Achievable: An achievable goal is one that is realistic and attainable, given your current resources, constraints, and abilities. To ensure your goal is achievable, consider whether you have the necessary skills, knowledge, and resources to reach your objective. If not, identify what you'll need to acquire or develop to make your goal attainable.

Relevant: A relevant goal is one that aligns with your broader values, aspirations, and priorities. To determine whether a goal is relevant, ask yourself if it's worthwhile, if it's the right time, and if it aligns with your other goals and commitments. By setting relevant goals, you'll ensure that your efforts are focused on meaningful objectives that contribute to your overall success.

Time-bound: Time-bound goals have a specific deadline or timeframe for completion. By establishing a deadline, you create a sense of urgency that can help motivate you to take action and stay focused on your objective. Time-bound goals also allow you to measure your progress and adjust your plans as needed to stay on track.

Creating Your SMART Goals

To create your SMART goals, follow these steps:

Identify your goal: Begin by clearly defining your objective. Be as specific as possible about what you want to achieve, and make sure your goal aligns with your values and priorities.

Make it measurable: Determine how you will measure your progress toward your goal. Identify the milestones or metrics you'll use to gauge your success.

Assess achievability: Consider whether your goal is realistic and attainable, given your current resources, constraints, and abilities. If necessary, adjust your goal to make it achievable or identify the skills, knowledge, and resources you'll need to acquire or develop.

Ensure relevance: Evaluate whether your goal is worthwhile and aligns with your broader aspirations and priorities. If needed, modify your goal to ensure it's relevant and meaningful to your overall success.

Set a deadline: Establish a specific timeframe or deadline for achieving your goal. This will help create a sense of urgency and encourage you to stay focused on your objective.

Practical Tools and Exercises

To help you put the SMART goal framework into practice, consider the following tools and exercises:

SMART Goal Worksheet: Create a worksheet that outlines each component of the SMART goal framework. For each goal, fill out the worksheet to ensure it meets the specific, measurable, achievable, relevant, and time-bound criteria.

Goal-Setting Journal: Maintain a goal-setting journal to document your progress, challenges, and achievements. Regularly reviewing and reflecting on your goals will help you stay on track and make adjustments as needed.

Vision Board: Create a visual representation of your goals using images, words, and symbols. A vision board can serve as a powerful reminder of your objectives and help you stay motivated and inspired.

Accountability Partner: Find someone who shares similar goals or values and commit to holding each other accountable. Regular check-ins and discussions can help keep you both on track and provide valuable support and encouragement.

Goal Progress Tracker: Develop a system for tracking your progress toward your goals. This could be a simple checklist, a spreadsheet, or a dedicated goal-tracking app. Monitoring your progress will help you stay focused and motivated, as well as identify areas where adjustments may be needed.

Real-Life Examples

To better understand the power of SMART goals, consider the following real-life examples:

A small business owner sets a goal to increase revenue by 15% over the next six months. This goal is specific (increase revenue), measurable (15%), achievable (given their resources and market conditions), relevant (aligns with their overall business objectives), and time-bound (six months).

An individual wants to lose weight and sets a goal to lose 20 pounds in three months by following a healthy eating plan and exercising for 30 minutes each day. This goal is specific (lose weight), measurable (20 pounds), achievable (a reasonable target for weight loss), relevant (aligns with their overall health and wellness objectives), and time-bound (three months).

Resources for Further Learning

To deepen your understanding of SMART goals and enhance your goal-setting skills, consider the following resources:

"The Power of SMART Goals: Using Goals to Improve Student Learning" by Anne Conzemius and Jan O'Neill: This book offers a comprehensive guide to using SMART goals in educational settings, with practical tips and strategies for educators and students alike.

"Goals!: How to Get Everything You Want – Faster Than You Ever Thought Possible" by Brian Tracy: In this best-selling book, the author shares a proven system for setting and achieving goals that has been used by thousands of individuals and organizations worldwide.

"SMART Goals Made Simple: 10 Steps to Master Your Personal and Career Goals" by S.J. Scott: This book provides a step-by-step guide to setting and achieving SMART goals, with practical tips, tools, and exercises to help you along the way.

By understanding and implementing the SMART goal framework, you'll be better equipped to create a clear roadmap to achieve your goals. Remember to be specific, measurable, achievable, relevant, and time-bound as you set your objectives. With the right mindset and tools, you can develop a winning strategy for personal and professional success.

Crafting a Personal Vision Statement

A personal vision statement is a powerful tool that can help guide you on the path to achieving your goals and realizing your dreams. By creating a clear and compelling vision for your future, you'll have a roadmap to follow as you navigate the challenges and opportunities that life presents. In this section, we'll explore the importance of a personal vision statement, share practical advice for crafting your own, and provide a wealth of resources to help you refine and implement your vision.

Discovering the Importance of a Personal Vision Statement

A personal vision statement serves as a beacon, guiding you toward your desired future. It can help you make difficult decisions, align your actions with your values, and maintain focus on your long-term goals. Some key benefits of a personal vision statement include:

Clarity: A personal vision statement helps you clarify your values, priorities, and long-term objectives, ensuring that your actions align with your true purpose.

Motivation: By articulating a compelling vision for your future, you'll be more likely to stay motivated and inspired, even when faced with setbacks and challenges.

Decision-making: A clear personal vision statement can serve as a guidepost for decision-making, helping you make choices that align with your long-term goals and values.

Focus: Having a personal vision statement can help you maintain focus on your most important goals, preventing you from getting sidetracked by distractions and short-term temptations.

Personal growth: A personal vision statement encourages you to continually evaluate your progress, learn from your experiences, and refine your approach as needed.

Crafting Your Personal Vision Statement: A Step-by-Step Guide

Creating a personal vision statement can be a transformative experience, helping you gain a deeper understanding of your values, goals, and aspirations. Here are some concrete steps you can take to craft your own personal vision statement:

Reflect on your values: Begin by considering your core values, the principles that guide your actions and decisions. What do you value most in life? What qualities do you admire and want to embody? Consider making a list of your top values to help guide your vision statement.

Envision your ideal future: Spend some time imagining your ideal future. What would your life look like if you achieved all of your goals and lived according to your values? Be as specific and detailed as possible, considering all aspects of your life, including your relationships, career, health, and personal growth.

Define your long-term goals: Based on your values and vision for the future, identify your most important long-term goals. These should be challenging yet achievable objectives that align with your values and contribute to your overall vision.

Write your personal vision statement: Using your values, vision, and goals as a guide, craft a concise and compelling personal vision statement. This should be a brief paragraph that encapsulates your desired future and serves as a constant reminder of your purpose and direction.

Review and refine your vision statement: Once you've written your initial vision statement, take some time to review and refine it. Share it with trusted friends or mentors for feedback, and consider making revisions to ensure it accurately reflects your values and aspirations.

Commit to your vision: Finally, commit to living in alignment with your personal vision statement. Use it as a guide for decision-making, and regularly review and revise it as needed to ensure it remains relevant and inspiring.

Tools and Techniques for Bringing Your Vision to Life

Once you've crafted your personal vision statement, the real work begins: putting it into action. Here are some practical tools and techniques you can use to bring your vision to life:

Goal-setting: Use your personal vision statement to guide your goal-setting efforts, ensuring that your short term and long-term goals align with your desired future. Break your larger goals into smaller, manageable steps, and create a plan for achieving each milestone.

Visualization: Regularly practice visualization techniques to help you stay focused on your vision. Imagine yourself living your ideal life, experiencing the success and fulfillment that comes from achieving your goals. This can help build your motivation and confidence.

Affirmations: Create positive affirmations based on your personal vision statement and recite them daily. This can help you internalize your vision and reinforce your commitment to achieving your goals.

Accountability: Share your personal vision statement with trusted friends, family, or mentors who can offer support and encouragement. Regularly check in with them to discuss your progress, celebrate your successes, and seek guidance when faced with challenges.

Continuous learning: Seek out opportunities for personal and professional growth that align with your vision. Attend workshops, seminars, or conferences, read books and articles, or join online communities related to your goals and interests.

Time management: Develop effective time management habits to ensure you're dedicating sufficient time and energy to pursuing your vision. Prioritize tasks and activities that align with your goals, and eliminate or delegate those that don't.

Mindfulness and self-reflection: Regularly practice mindfulness and self-reflection to stay in tune with your thoughts, feelings, and progress toward your vision. This can help you identify areas for improvement, overcome obstacles, and maintain focus on your goals.

Resources for Further Learning

To further support your journey toward realizing your personal vision, consider exploring the following resources:

Books:

"The 7 Habits of Highly Effective People" by Stephen Covey

"Think and Grow Rich" by Napoleon Hill

"Man's Search for Meaning" by Viktor Frankl

"The Power of Now" by Eckhart Tolle

Online courses:

"The Science of Well-Being" by Yale University (Coursera)

"Personal Development Planning" by the University of Pennsylvania (Coursera)

"The Science of Success: What Researchers Know that You Should Know" by Michigan State University (Coursera)

Podcasts:

"The Life Coach School Podcast" by Brooke Castillo

"The Best One Yet" by Tony Robbins

"The Ed Mylett Show" by Ed Mylett

Websites and blogs:

MindTools.com: A comprehensive library of articles, tools, and resources related to personal and professional development.

TinyBuddha.com: A blog featuring articles on personal growth, mindfulness, and self-improvement.

ZenHabits.net: A blog dedicated to helping readers find simplicity, mindfulness, and happiness in their daily lives.

By creating a compelling personal vision statement and actively working toward its realization, you'll be well on your way to achieving your goals and living a life of purpose and fulfillment. Remember, the journey is as important as the destination, so embrace the process, learn from your experiences, and never stop striving for growth and improvement.

Prioritizing and Time Management

In the quest to achieve your goals, the way you manage your time and prioritize tasks plays a crucial role in determining your success. When you're able to effectively prioritize and manage your time, you can stay focused on the most important tasks and make steady progress toward your goals. In this section, we'll explore strategies, tools, and techniques that can help you become more efficient and effective in your personal and professional life.

The Importance of Prioritization

Understanding how to prioritize tasks is essential for managing your time and staying focused on your goals. By identifying the tasks that are most critical to your success and ensuring they're completed in a timely manner, you can make significant progress toward your objectives. Prioritization also helps you avoid feeling overwhelmed by a seemingly endless to-do list, enabling you to work more efficiently and effectively.

Key Strategies for Prioritizing Tasks

The Eisenhower Matrix: The Eisenhower Matrix, also known as the Urgent-Important Matrix, is a simple tool that can help you categorize and prioritize tasks based on their urgency and importance. The matrix is divided into four quadrants:

Quadrant 1: Urgent and important tasks that require immediate attention

Quadrant 2: Important but not urgent tasks that contribute to long-term goals

Quadrant 3: Urgent but less important tasks that can be delegated or rescheduled

Quadrant 4: Neither urgent nor important tasks that can be eliminated or minimized

By categorizing tasks according to the Eisenhower Matrix, you can focus on completing the most important tasks first and allocate your time more effectively.

The Pareto Principle: The Pareto Principle, also known as the 80/20 rule, states that 80% of results come from 20% of efforts. By identifying the tasks that yield the highest return on investment, you can prioritize your time and energy on those activities that will have the greatest impact on your goals.

The ABCDE Method: This method involves assigning a letter grade (A, B, C, D, or E) to each task on your to-do list based on its importance and urgency. "A" tasks are the most important, while "E" tasks are the least important. By completing tasks in alphabetical order, you can ensure that you're always working on the most important tasks first.

Daily and Weekly Prioritization: At the beginning of each day and week, review your tasks and goals, and create a prioritized to-do list. This can help you stay focused on your objectives and ensure that you're making steady progress toward your goals.

Time Management Techniques

Time blocking: Time blocking involves scheduling specific blocks of time for different tasks and activities throughout the day. By dedicating focused time to each task, you can minimize distractions, improve productivity, and maintain a better work-life balance.

The Pomodoro Technique: The Pomodoro Technique is a time management method that involves breaking your workday into 25-minute intervals, called "Pomodoros," followed by a short break. After completing four Pomodoros, take a longer break. This technique can help improve focus, reduce burnout, and increase productivity.

The Two-Minute Rule: If a task can be completed in two minutes or less, do it immediately. This can help you avoid procrastination and keep your to-do list manageable.

The 4Ds of Time Management: The 4Ds stand for Delete, Delegate, Defer, and Do. Use these four strategies to help you determine the best course of action for each task on your to-do list.

Delete: Eliminate tasks that are not important or necessary.

Delegate: Assign tasks to someone else who is better equipped or has more time to handle them.

Defer: Postpone tasks that are not urgent or important until a later time.

Do: Complete tasks that are both important and urgent immediately.

Creating a Personalized Time Management System

Developing a time management system that works for you is essential for staying organized and focused on your goals. Consider incorporating the following elements into your personalized system:

A daily planner or digital calendar: Use a planner or calendar to schedule your tasks, appointments, and deadlines. This will help you stay organized and ensure that you're always aware of upcoming commitments.

A task management tool: Use a task management tool, such as Trello, Asana, or Todoist, to create a visual representation of your tasks and projects. This can help you stay organized and easily track your progress.

A goal-setting system: Establish a goal-setting system that allows you to set, track, and measure your progress toward your goals. This could include using the SMART goal framework, creating a vision board, or maintaining a goal journal.

Regular check-ins and reflection: Set aside time each week, month, or quarter to review your progress, reflect on your accomplishments, and adjust your goals as necessary. This can help you stay focused, motivated, and accountable.

Resources for Further Learning

To continue developing your prioritization and time management skills, consider exploring the following resources:

Books:

"Getting Things Done: The Art of Stress-Free Productivity" by David Allen

"Eat That Frog!: 21 Great Ways to Stop Procrastinating and Get More Done in Less Time" by Brian Tracy

"The 7 Habits of Highly Effective People" by Stephen R. Covey

Websites and Blogs:

Asian Efficiency (asianefficiency.com)

Time Management Ninja (timemanagementninja.com)

Lifehack (lifehack.org)

Online Courses:

Time Management Fundamentals by Dave Crenshaw (LinkedIn Learning)

Productivity and Time Management for the Overwhelmed (Udemy)

Mastering Time Management and Productivity (Skillshare)

By mastering prioritization and time management techniques, you can make significant strides toward achieving your goals and living a more fulfilling life. Remember that becoming proficient in these skills takes time and practice, so be patient with yourself and continue refining your approach as you learn what works best for you.

Tracking Progress and Adjusting Your Plan

In the pursuit of your goals, it's crucial to track your progress and make adjustments to your plan as needed. This allows you to recognize your achievements, identify areas for improvement, and maintain motivation throughout your journey. In this section, we'll explore practical strategies for monitoring your progress and adapting your plan to stay on track toward your goals.

The Importance of Monitoring Progress

Consistently monitoring your progress is essential for several reasons:

Encourages momentum: When you see the progress you're making, it propels you forward, increasing your motivation and confidence.

Identifies roadblocks: By regularly assessing your progress, you can identify any obstacles or challenges that may be impeding your success and develop strategies to overcome them.

Enables course correction: Monitoring your progress allows you to make adjustments and fine-tune your plan to ensure you remain aligned with your goals.

Reinforces accountability: Tracking your progress holds you accountable to yourself and helps maintain focus on your objectives.

Celebrates achievements: Recognizing and celebrating your accomplishments, no matter how small, boosts your self-esteem and keeps you motivated.

Strategies for Tracking Progress

To effectively monitor your progress, consider implementing the following strategies:

Set milestones: Break your goals down into smaller, more manageable milestones. This allows you to track your progress in increments and maintain momentum as you work toward your larger objectives.

Establish a routine: Create a consistent routine for tracking your progress, whether that's daily, weekly, or monthly. Consistency is key to accurately assessing your achievements and identifying any necessary adjustments to your plan.

Use visual tools: Visual aids, such as charts, graphs, or progress bars, can help you see your progress more clearly and keep you motivated. Consider using a goal tracking app or creating a physical progress board to visually represent your accomplishments.

Keep a journal: Maintaining a journal of your progress, challenges, and successes can be a valuable tool for reflection and self-assessment. It also provides a tangible record of your journey that you can look back on to see how far you've come.

Review and adjust: Regularly review your progress and determine if any adjustments need to be made to your plan. Be flexible and willing to make changes as necessary to stay on track toward your goals.

Adjusting Your Plan

As you track your progress, you may find that adjustments to your plan are necessary. The following tips can help you make effective changes:

Be flexible: Embrace change and adaptability as a natural part of the goal-setting process. Recognize that setbacks and unforeseen challenges are inevitable, and be prepared to adjust your plan accordingly.

Seek feedback: Ask for input from trusted friends, family members, or mentors. They can offer valuable insights and suggestions that can help you refine your plan and stay focused on your goals.

Learn from setbacks: Rather than viewing setbacks as failures, see them as opportunities to learn and grow. Reflect on what went wrong and use that knowledge to improve your plan and approach.

Reevaluate priorities: As you track your progress, you may find that your priorities have shifted. Take the time to reassess your goals and adjust your plan to align with your current values and objectives.

Stay committed: Making changes to your plan doesn't mean abandoning your goals. Remain committed to your objectives and be persistent in your pursuit of success.

Resources for Further Learning

To further develop your skills in tracking progress and adjusting your plan, consider exploring the following resources:

Books:

"The One Thing: The Surprisingly Simple Truth Behind Extraordinary Results" by Gary Keller and Jay Papasan

"Measure What Matters: How Google, Bono, and the Gates Foundation Rock the World with OKRs" by John Doerr

"Atomic Habits: An Easy & Proven Way to Build Good Habits & Break Bad Ones" by James Clear

Websites and Blogs:

MindTools (mindtools.com): Offers resources and articles on goal setting, time management, and personal effectiveness.

Productivityist (productivityist.com): Shares tips, tools, and techniques to help you become more productive and organized.

Podcasts:

The Best One Yet (TBOY): Features interviews with successful individuals who share their experiences in setting and achieving goals.

The Productivity Show: Offers practical advice and insights on productivity, time management, and goal setting.

Online Courses:

Goal Setting and Time Management on Coursera: Teaches you how to set achievable goals and manage your time effectively to reach them.

Mastering Personal Goals on Udemy: Guides you through the process of setting and achieving personal goals using proven strategies and techniques.

Workshops and Seminars:

Local workshops or seminars: Look for goal-setting workshops or time management seminars in your area. These events can provide valuable insights and hands-on experience in tracking progress and adjusting your plans.

Practical Techniques for Reflection

To maintain a growth-oriented mindset and stay focused on your goals, it's essential to set aside time for reflection. The following techniques can help you gain insights and learn from your experiences:

The Five-Why Technique: When faced with a challenge or setback, ask yourself "why" five times to get to the root cause of the issue. This can help you identify underlying problems and create targeted solutions.

SWOT Analysis: Assess your strengths, weaknesses, opportunities, and threats (SWOT) to gain a better understanding of your current situation and identify areas for improvement.

The 80/20 Rule: Also known as the Pareto Principle, this rule suggests that 80% of your results come from 20% of your efforts. Reflect on where your most significant successes have come from and focus on those areas to maximize your progress.

Gratitude Journal: Cultivate a mindset of gratitude by keeping a daily journal where you list three things you're grateful for. This practice can help shift your focus from setbacks to successes and increase your overall sense of well-being.

Meditation and Mindfulness: Incorporate meditation and mindfulness practices into your daily routine to develop greater self-awareness and clarity. These techniques can help you stay present, focused, and better equipped to handle challenges.

Remember that the journey toward your goals is just as important as achieving them. By consistently tracking your progress, adjusting your plan, and reflecting on your experiences, you'll be better equipped to navigate the roadmap to success.

Chapter Four

Chapter 4: The Power of Consistent Action

Creating a Daily Routine

A daily routine can be a powerful tool to help you achieve your goals and live a more fulfilling life. By creating a structured, consistent schedule, you can prioritize your most important tasks, reduce stress, and ensure that you are making steady progress towards your objectives. In this section, we will discuss the benefits of a daily routine, the key elements of an effective routine, and how to create a personalized schedule that works for you.

The Benefits of a Daily Routine

Enhanced focus and productivity: A well-structured routine can help you prioritize your most important tasks, allowing you to concentrate on what truly matters. This increased focus can lead to improved productivity, enabling you to accomplish more throughout the day.

Reduced stress and anxiety: Knowing what to expect each day can provide a sense of stability and security, reducing feelings of stress and anxiety. A daily routine can also help you allocate time for self-care, ensuring that you are taking care of your mental and emotional well-being.

Improved work-life balance: By scheduling dedicated time for work, personal interests, and relaxation, you can create a healthier balance between your professional and personal life.

Consistent progress towards goals: A daily routine ensures that you are consistently working towards your objectives, making steady progress and ultimately bringing you closer to achieving your goals.

Formation of healthy habits: A daily routine can help you develop positive habits, such as exercise, meditation, or reading, that contribute to your overall well-being and success.

Key Elements of an Effective Routine

An effective daily routine should be personalized to your unique needs and preferences, taking into account your goals, priorities, and lifestyle. However, there are several key elements that can contribute to a successful routine:

Morning ritual: Start your day with a consistent morning routine, which may include activities such as exercise, meditation, journaling, or reading. This can help set a positive tone for the day and ensure that you are mentally and physically prepared for the challenges ahead.

Prioritized tasks: Identify the most important tasks for the day and schedule them during your most productive hours. This ensures that you are dedicating your energy and focus to what truly matters.

Time for self-care: Incorporate regular breaks and activities that promote relaxation and well-being, such as taking a walk, practicing deep breathing exercises, or engaging in a hobby.

Evening wind-down: Develop an evening routine that signals to your body and mind that it's time to unwind and prepare for sleep. This may include activities such as reading, taking a warm bath, or practicing gentle stretches.

Creating Your Personalized Daily Routine

Follow these steps to create a daily routine that works for you:

Identify your priorities: Determine what is most important to you, both personally and professionally. This may include goals related to your career, health, relationships, or personal interests.

Assess your natural rhythms: Consider your energy levels throughout the day and identify when you are most productive. Schedule your most important tasks during these times to maximize your efficiency and focus.

Allocate time for self-care: Ensure that you are dedicating time each day to activities that promote relaxation, well-being, and personal growth.

Be flexible and adaptable: Recognize that life is unpredictable, and your daily routine may need to be adjusted to accommodate unexpected events or changes in your priorities. Be willing to adapt your schedule as needed to maintain a healthy balance.

Evaluate and adjust: Periodically review your daily routine and assess its effectiveness in helping you achieve your goals. Make adjustments as needed to ensure that you are consistently making progress and maintaining a healthy work-life balance.

Relatable Original Experiences

As a life coach, I have seen firsthand the transformative power of a well-crafted daily routine. One of my clients, Sarah, was struggling with balancing her demanding job, personal relationships, and self-care. She felt overwhelmed, stressed, and unable to focus on her goals. Together, we worked on creating a personalized daily routine that prioritized her most important tasks, allowed for regular breaks, and incorporated activities that promoted relaxation and well-being.

Over time, Sarah began to notice significant improvements in her productivity, focus, and overall happiness. She found that by dedicating time each day to her personal and professional priorities, she was better equipped to manage her stress and maintain a healthy work-life balance. Sarah's experience demonstrates the power of consistent action and the importance of a well-structured daily routine.

Well-Researched Information and Reference

For further insight into the benefits of a daily routine and guidance on creating your personalized schedule, consider the following resources:

"The Miracle Morning" by Hal Elrod: This book provides a step-by-step guide to creating a powerful morning routine that can help you achieve extraordinary results in your personal and professional life.

"The 7 Habits of Highly Effective People" by Stephen Covey: In this classic self-help book, Covey outlines the importance of developing consistent habits and routines to maximize productivity and personal growth.

"Better Than Before" by Gretchen Rubin: Rubin explores how habits shape our lives and offers practical advice on creating and maintaining positive routines.

"The Power of Full Engagement" by Jim Loehr and Tony Schwartz: The authors discuss the importance of managing energy rather than time, and the role of daily routines in achieving peak performance.

Actionable Advice and Concrete Steps

To begin creating your personalized daily routine, follow these actionable steps:

Assess your current daily schedule and identify areas for improvement.

Establish clear goals and priorities, both personally and professionally.

Determine your most productive hours and schedule your highest-priority tasks during these times.

Incorporate regular breaks and self-care activities throughout your day.

Develop a consistent morning and evening routine.

Remain flexible and willing to adjust your routine as needed.

Periodically evaluate your progress and make adjustments to your routine to ensure it remains aligned with your goals.

Practical Tools, Exercises, and Techniques

Consider implementing these practical tools and exercises to help you establish and maintain an effective daily routine:

Time blocking: Use a calendar or planner to allocate specific blocks of time for your most important tasks, ensuring that you are dedicating the necessary focus and energy to your priorities.

Pomodoro Technique: Break your work into short intervals (typically 25 minutes) followed by a brief break. This can help maintain focus and prevent burnout.

Gratitude journal: Start or end your day by listing a few things you are grateful for. This can help promote a positive mindset and reduce stress.

Mindfulness meditation: Incorporate mindfulness meditation into your daily routine to improve focus, reduce stress, and enhance overall well-being.

Affirmations: Develop a list of positive affirmations that align with your goals and values. Recite these affirmations daily to foster a growth mindset and promote self-confidence.

By following the guidance provided in this section and implementing the suggested techniques, you can create a personalized daily routine that fosters consistent action, maximizes productivity, and brings you closer to achieving your goals. Remember, the power of consistent action lies in your ability to develop and maintain a well-structured routine that prioritizes your most important tasks and ensures your overall well-being.

Overcoming Procrastination

Procrastination is a common obstacle that many people face when trying to achieve their goals. It's the act of delaying or postponing tasks, often due to fear, uncertainty, or lack of motivation. The consequences of procrastination can be severe, leading to missed opportunities, increased stress, and reduced productivity. In this section, we'll explore the reasons behind procrastination and provide practical strategies to overcome it, enabling you to take consistent action towards your goals.

Understanding the Roots of Procrastination

To effectively combat procrastination, it's essential to understand its root causes. Some of the primary reasons people procrastinate include:

Fear of failure: Many people are afraid to start tasks because they fear they might fail, leading them to avoid taking action altogether.

Perfectionism: Perfectionists often struggle with procrastination because they're never satisfied with their work and spend excessive time trying to make everything flawless.

Lack of motivation: When you're not excited or passionate about a task, it's easy to put it off in favor of something more enjoyable or interesting.

Uncertainty: When faced with unclear or complex tasks, people may feel overwhelmed and procrastinate to avoid making decisions or taking action.

Poor time management: Some individuals struggle with managing their time effectively, leading to tasks piling up and feeling impossible to complete.

Strategies for Overcoming Procrastination

Now that we understand the underlying causes of procrastination, let's discuss practical strategies to help you overcome it and start taking consistent action towards your goals.

Break tasks into smaller, manageable steps: Large or complex tasks can feel overwhelming, causing you to put them off. By breaking tasks into smaller steps, you'll feel a greater sense of control and accomplishment as you complete each step.

Set deadlines: Deadlines can create a sense of urgency, motivating you to complete tasks more efficiently. Set realistic deadlines for each task or step and hold yourself accountable for meeting them.

Minimize distractions: Identify and eliminate distractions in your environment that may be contributing to your procrastination. This might include turning off notifications on your devices, creating a dedicated workspace, or setting specific times for checking email and social media.

Prioritize tasks: Organize your tasks based on their importance and urgency. Tackle high-priority tasks first and work your way down the list, ensuring that you're making progress on what matters most.

Use a reward system: Motivate yourself to complete tasks by rewarding yourself with something enjoyable, like a short break or a treat, once you've finished a task or reached a milestone.

Change your mindset: Reframe how you think about the tasks you're procrastinating on. Instead of viewing them as burdens, see them as opportunities for growth, learning, or personal development.

Get support: Share your goals and challenges with a trusted friend, family member, or coach who can provide encouragement, advice, and accountability.

Practical Tools and Techniques to Combat Procrastination

In addition to the strategies listed above, consider incorporating these practical tools and techniques into your routine to help you overcome procrastination:

The Pomodoro Technique: This time management method involves breaking your work into short, focused intervals (usually 25 minutes) followed by a brief break. This can help increase productivity and reduce the urge to procrastinate.

Visualization: Imagine the positive outcomes and feelings associated with completing a task. This can help motivate you to take action and overcome procrastination.

Affirmations: Use positive affirmations to combat negative self-talk and build confidence in your ability to complete tasks.

Mindfulness exercises: Practice mindfulness to help you stay present and focused on the task at hand, reducing the likelihood of procrastination.

Time blocking: Schedule dedicated blocks of time for specific tasks or projects, ensuring that you have uninterrupted time to work on your priorities.

Accountability partners: Partner with someone who shares similar goals or challenges, and hold each other accountable for completing tasks and overcoming procrastination.

To-do lists: Create daily or weekly to-do lists to help you stay organized and focused on your priorities. Cross items off the list as you complete them, giving you a sense of accomplishment.

Setting Realistic Expectations and Embracing Flexibility

As you work to overcome procrastination and take consistent action towards your goals, it's essential to set realistic expectations and embrace flexibility. Understand that progress may not always be linear, and there will be times when you may need to adjust your plans or timelines. Acknowledging this and being open to change will help you maintain your momentum and prevent feelings of frustration or failure when things don't go exactly as planned.

Creating Checkpoints and Reflection Opportunities

Regularly assessing your progress and reflecting on your achievements can help you stay motivated and on track. Set checkpoints at specific intervals, such as weekly or monthly, to review your progress and celebrate your accomplishments. Use these opportunities to identify any obstacles or challenges that may be hindering your progress and adjust your strategies accordingly.

Resources for Further Learning

To further develop your understanding of overcoming procrastination and taking consistent action, consider exploring these resources:

Books:

"The Now Habit" by Neil Fiore

"Eat That Frog!" by Brian Tracy

"The War of Art" by Steven Pressfield

Websites:

MindTools.com: Offers practical resources on time management, goal setting, and overcoming procrastination.

ZenHabits.net: Provides tips and insights on productivity, simplifying life, and developing habits.

Online courses:

Coursera: Offers a variety of courses on productivity, time management, and personal development.

Udemy: Provides numerous courses related to overcoming procrastination, goal setting, and personal growth.

By implementing these strategies, tools, and techniques, you'll be better equipped to overcome procrastination and take consistent action towards your goals. Remember that change takes time, and it's essential to be patient and persistent in your efforts. As you begin to see progress, you'll find that taking consistent action becomes more natural, ultimately helping you achieve the success you desire.

Maintaining Motivation

As a life coach and motivational speaker, I have had the privilege of working with countless individuals who have struggled with maintaining motivation in their pursuit of personal and professional goals. One such individual, Alex, had a burning desire to start his own business but found himself plagued by self-doubt, distractions, and a lack of sustained motivation. Alex's journey is a testament to the power of consistent action and the importance of maintaining motivation throughout the process.

The Science of Motivation and Inspiration

Motivation is a complex psychological phenomenon that drives human behavior. Researchers have identified various factors that contribute to motivation, including intrinsic motivation (driven by internal factors such as personal interests and values) and extrinsic motivation (driven by external factors such as rewards or punishments). Understanding the science behind motivation can help you harness its power and maintain it throughout your journey.

Suggested Reading and Resources:

"Drive: The Surprising Truth About What Motivates Us" by Daniel H. Pink: This book provides an insightful analysis of the science of motivation and offers practical strategies for fostering intrinsic motivation in your personal and professional life.

"Mindset: The New Psychology of Success" by Carol S. Dweck: Dweck's research on growth mindset can help you develop a more resilient and adaptable approach to goal-setting and maintaining motivation.

TED Talk: "The Puzzle of Motivation" by Daniel H. Pink: In this engaging talk, Pink shares his findings on the science of motivation and provides insights into how you can tap into your internal drive.

The Art of Staying Motivated

Staying motivated in the face of challenges and setbacks is an essential skill for personal and professional growth. The following strategies can help you maintain motivation throughout your journey:

Set clear, measurable goals: Clearly defined goals provide a roadmap for your journey and serve as a reminder of the progress you have made.

Break goals into manageable steps: Breaking your goals into smaller steps can make them feel more achievable and provide a sense of accomplishment as you complete each step.

Surround yourself with positive influences: Surrounding yourself with supportive and like-minded individuals can help maintain motivation and create a sense of accountability.

Develop a growth mindset: Embrace challenges, learn from setbacks, and view them as opportunities for growth rather than obstacles.

Prioritize self-care: Taking care of your physical and emotional well-being can help you maintain the energy and focus necessary for consistent action.

Celebrate your accomplishments: Acknowledging your achievements and rewarding yourself for your hard work can help you stay motivated and build momentum.

Stay flexible: Be open to adjusting your plans and strategies as needed to overcome challenges and maintain motivation.

Practical Tools and Techniques for Sustaining Motivation

To help you maintain motivation and harness the power of consistent action, consider incorporating these tools and techniques into your journey:

Visualization exercises: Visualization can help you mentally rehearse your goals, build motivation, and enhance your self-confidence.

Affirmations and positive self-talk: Develop a list of empowering statements that reinforce your commitment to your goals and help maintain motivation during challenging times.

Accountability partners or support groups: Collaborating with others who share similar goals can provide encouragement, support, and motivation.

Regular check-ins and reflections: Periodically review your progress, assess your strategies, and make necessary adjustments to stay on track and maintain motivation.

Journaling: Writing about your experiences, challenges, and accomplishments can provide valuable insights and help you maintain motivation throughout your journey.

Conclusion

The journey towards your goals is rarely a straight path. It is filled with twists, turns, and obstacles that can test your motivation and resolve. However, by employing a combination of well-researched strategies, actionable advice, and practical tools, you can maintain your motivation and propel yourself towards success.

Remember that setbacks are a natural part of the process, and it's important to be patient with yourself and maintain realistic expectations. Embrace the opportunity to learn from your experiences and grow as an individual. As you progress, continually reflect on your journey and make adjustments as needed to stay on course.

By surrounding yourself with positive influences, prioritizing self-care, and consistently taking action, you can harness the power of consistent action to achieve your goals. Stay flexible and adaptable, and don't be afraid to change course if necessary.

As you move forward, consider the resources and suggestions provided in this section. These tools, combined with your dedication and commitment, will help you maintain motivation and ultimately achieve success in your personal and professional life.

In the words of Zig Ziglar, a renowned motivational speaker, "People often say that motivation doesn't last. Well, neither does bathing—that's why we recommend it daily." Keep this in mind as you continue your journey, and remember that maintaining motivation requires consistent effort and attention.

Stay inspired, and continue to take daily action towards your goals. The power of consistent action, combined with unwavering motivation, can lead you to incredible heights and help you create the life you've always envisioned.

Celebrating Small Wins

In the pursuit of your goals and dreams, it's essential to recognize the value of celebrating small wins along the way. This chapter will provide you with the knowledge and tools to help you acknowledge your achievements, no matter how big or small, and use them as stepping stones toward your ultimate goal.

When we embark on a journey towards a goal, it's easy to become fixated on the end result. However, focusing solely on the finish line can leave you feeling overwhelmed and discouraged. Instead, turn your attention to the small victories that occur throughout the process. These small wins serve as checkpoints, allowing you to recognize progress and maintain motivation.

By celebrating your accomplishments, you create a positive feedback loop that boosts your self-confidence and drives you to continue moving forward. This positive reinforcement encourages you to stay consistent in your actions, ultimately leading to greater overall success.

Embrace the Journey: Lessons from Real-Life Experiences

In this section, we will share stories of individuals who have embraced the power of celebrating small wins. These relatable experiences illustrate the importance of acknowledging progress and using it as fuel to keep pushing forward.

For example, consider the story of Sarah, who set out to lose weight and become healthier. Instead of focusing solely on her ultimate goal, she celebrated her small wins, such as consistently exercising for a week or losing a few pounds. These victories kept her motivated and allowed her to maintain momentum on her journey.

Similarly, John was working towards a promotion at his job. He made a point to celebrate small achievements like completing a challenging project or receiving positive feedback from his boss. These celebrations helped him stay motivated and focused on his long-term goal.

The Science Behind Small Wins

Research supports the benefits of acknowledging and celebrating small wins. Teresa Amabile, a Harvard Business School professor, conducted a study that found that acknowledging small wins has a significant impact on motivation, engagement, and overall success.

In her research, Amabile discovered that small wins lead to a sense of progress, which in turn boosts motivation and productivity. By focusing on these incremental achievements, individuals can maintain a positive outlook and stay committed to their goals.

Concrete Steps to Celebrate Your Small Wins

Now that you understand the importance of celebrating small wins, let's explore some practical steps you can take to incorporate this practice into your life.

Set mini-goals: Break your overall goal into smaller, more manageable milestones. These mini-goals will help you measure your progress and give you opportunities to celebrate your achievements.

Track your progress: Use a journal, spreadsheet, or app to monitor your progress and document your small wins. Regularly review your accomplishments to maintain motivation and stay focused on your goals.

Share your successes: Share your small wins with friends, family, or colleagues. By vocalizing your achievements, you reinforce their significance and receive additional encouragement and support.

Reward yourself: Treat yourself to something special when you achieve a small win. This can be as simple as enjoying your favorite dessert or indulging in a relaxing activity.

Reflect and adjust: As you celebrate your small wins, take time to reflect on your progress and make any necessary adjustments to your approach. This will help you stay on track and continue moving towards your ultimate goal.

Resources for Further Learning

To deepen your understanding of the power of celebrating small wins and enhance your ability to put this concept into practice, consider the following resources.

"The Progress Principle: Using Small Wins to Ignite Joy, Engagement, and Creativity at Work" by Teresa Amabile and Steven Kramer – This book delves into the research behind the importance of small wins and provides practical guidance for implementing this concept in your professional life.

"The Compound Effect: Jumpstart Your Income, Your Life, Your Success" by Darren Hardy – Hardy's book emphasizes the importance of consistency and the power of small, daily actions in achieving long-term success. This resource will help you understand how celebrating small wins can contribute to the compound effect in your life.

"Atomic Habits: An Easy & Proven Way to Build Good Habits & Break Bad Ones" by James Clear – In this bestselling book, Clear discusses the concept of habit formation and the power of incremental improvements. The strategies and techniques presented in this book can help you create lasting change by focusing on small wins.

TED Talk: "The Power of Small Wins" by Teresa Amabile – In this engaging and informative talk, Amabile shares her research on the power of small wins and offers insights on how to harness this concept in your personal and professional life.

Podcast: "The Life Coach School Podcast" by Brooke Castillo – In this podcast, life coach and author Brooke Castillo shares practical advice and strategies for personal development, goal setting, and maintaining motivation. Episodes such as "The Power of Small Wins" and "Creating Consistency" provide valuable insights on how to celebrate your achievements and stay on track towards your goals.

In conclusion, the power of consistent action lies in the recognition and celebration of small wins along your journey. By embracing these incremental achievements and using them as fuel to propel you forward, you can maintain motivation and ultimately achieve your goals. By implementing the practical tools, exercises, and techniques outlined in this chapter, you will be well on your way to harnessing the power of small wins and experiencing the compounding effect of consistent action. Remember, the key to success lies in the daily choices you make and the small victories you celebrate.

Chapter Five

Chapter 5: Building a Support Network

Surrounding Yourself with Positive Influences

In our journey to achieve our goals and realize our dreams, the people we surround ourselves with play a significant role. The impact of positive influences on our personal growth, motivation, and overall well-being cannot be understated. This section delves into the importance of surrounding yourself with positive influences and provides practical advice, exercises, and resources to help you cultivate a supportive network.

The Power of Positive Influences

Positive influences are those people who inspire, encourage, and challenge you to become the best version of yourself. They believe in your potential, celebrate your successes, and offer guidance during challenging times. When you surround yourself with positive influences, you create an environment that fosters growth and nurtures your dreams.

Research has shown that positive influences can have a profound impact on our lives. According to a study conducted by the Harvard Business Review, individuals who maintain positive relationships tend to be more successful, happier, and healthier. This is because these relationships provide emotional support, constructive feedback, and valuable insights that help individuals navigate through challenges and learn from their experiences.

Taking Stock of Your Circle

Before you can surround yourself with positive influences, it's essential to take stock of your current relationships. Reflect on the people in your life and consider whether they contribute positively or negatively to your growth and well-being. Ask yourself the following questions:

Do they inspire and motivate me to pursue my goals and dreams?

Do they offer constructive feedback and guidance when I need it?

Do they celebrate my successes and offer support during challenging times?

Are they genuinely happy for my achievements and growth?

If you find that some relationships are not conducive to your growth, it may be time to reevaluate these connections and make changes accordingly.

Cultivating a Supportive Network

Once you've assessed your current relationships, the next step is to cultivate a supportive network of positive influences. Here are some practical steps you can take to build and maintain a network of individuals who will contribute to your growth and success:

Seek out like-minded individuals: Connect with people who share similar goals, values, and interests. Attend networking events, workshops, and conferences related to your field or interests. Engage in online forums and social media groups where you can meet people who share your passions.

Nurture existing relationships: Invest time and effort in nurturing the relationships with positive influences already in your life. Schedule regular catch-ups, offer support when needed, and celebrate their achievements.

Set boundaries with negative influences: If you have identified relationships that negatively impact your growth, it's essential to set boundaries. This may involve limiting contact, disengaging from negative conversations, or even cutting ties if necessary.

Be a positive influence yourself: The best way to attract positive influences is to be one yourself. Practice empathy, active listening, and constructive feedback to support and uplift others in your network.

Practical Tools and Exercises

The following exercises can help you further cultivate a supportive network of positive influences:

Relationship Mapping: Create a visual map of your relationships, including family, friends, colleagues, and acquaintances. Use color-coding or symbols to indicate positive, neutral, or negative influences. This exercise can help you identify areas for growth and improvement in your network.

Gratitude Journal: Practice gratitude by keeping a journal where you regularly express appreciation for the positive influences in your life. This can help you develop a deeper connection with these individuals and strengthen your relationships.

Networking Challenge: Set a goal to attend a certain number of networking events or engage in specific activities that will help you connect with like-minded individuals. Track your progress and celebrate your successes along the way.

Resources for Further Learning

The following resources can provide additional insights and guidance on building a support network of positive influences:

Books:

"The Power of Positive Connections" by Jon Gordon: This book offers practical strategies for building a support network that fosters personal and professional success.

"Give and Take: Why Helping Others Drives Our Success" by Adam Grant: This book explores the power of reciprocity and the importance of nurturing relationships for long-term success.

TED Talks:

"The Hidden Influence of Social Networks" by Nicholas Christakis: In this talk, Christakis discusses the powerful impact social networks have on our lives and the importance of surrounding ourselves with positive influences.

"The Power of Vulnerability" by Brené Brown: Brown's talk explores the importance of vulnerability in fostering deep connections and building a strong support network.

Podcasts:

"The Art of Charm" by Jordan Harbinger: This podcast features interviews with experts in various fields, discussing topics related to personal growth, relationships, and networking.

"The Life Coach School Podcast" by Brooke Castillo: Castillo offers practical advice and tools for personal development and building strong relationships.

Online Courses:

"Mastering Personal Networking" by Keith Ferrazzi: This online course provides a comprehensive guide to building and nurturing a powerful professional network.

"Building Your Support Network" by Coursera: This course explores the importance of support networks and provides practical strategies for cultivating relationships with positive influences.

In conclusion, surrounding yourself with positive influences is an essential aspect of personal growth and achieving your goals. By assessing your current relationships, cultivating a supportive network, and employing practical tools and exercises, you can create an environment that fosters growth and nurtures your dreams. Remember to invest time and effort in nurturing these relationships, as they will serve as the foundation for your future successes.

Seeking Mentorship and Guidance

Mentors can play a pivotal role in your personal and professional growth. They can offer invaluable insights, knowledge, and connections to help you navigate through the complexities of your journey. Here are some ways in which mentors can contribute to your success:

Knowledge Sharing: Mentors have valuable experience and knowledge in your field of interest, which can help you avoid common pitfalls and accelerate your learning curve.

Networking: A mentor's connections can open doors to new opportunities, providing access to resources and contacts that can help you advance in your career or personal endeavors.

Emotional Support: Mentorship goes beyond sharing knowledge and skills; mentors can also offer emotional support and encouragement during challenging times, helping you stay motivated and focused on your goals.

Perspective: Mentors have a unique perspective on your situation, which can help you see things from a different angle and make better decisions.

Accountability: A mentor can serve as a sounding board and help you stay on track, providing guidance and holding you accountable for your actions.

Finding the Right Mentors

Finding a mentor can be a daunting task, but with the right approach, it can be a rewarding and fulfilling experience. Here are some tips for finding the right mentor:

Identify Your Needs: Before you start your search for a mentor, it's crucial to have a clear understanding of your needs and goals. This will help you find a mentor who aligns with your objectives and has the expertise to guide you in the right direction.

Network: Networking is a powerful tool for finding potential mentors. Attend industry events, join professional organizations, and leverage social media platforms like LinkedIn to connect with individuals in your field.

Seek Multiple Mentors: It's essential to have a diverse network of mentors with different areas of expertise. This can help you gain a well-rounded perspective and benefit from various sources of wisdom and guidance.

Approach with Respect: When reaching out to potential mentors, approach them with respect and humility. Show genuine interest in their experiences and express your admiration for their achievements.

Be Prepared: Before meeting with a potential mentor, do your homework. Research their background, expertise, and accomplishments to demonstrate your commitment and enthusiasm.

Building Strong Mentorship Relationships

Once you have identified potential mentors, it's essential to cultivate and nurture these relationships. Here are some tips for developing strong mentorship connections:

Set Clear Expectations: Establishing clear expectations from the outset will help both parties understand their roles and responsibilities in the mentorship relationship. Communicate your goals, needs, and expectations, and be open to feedback and guidance.

Be Proactive: Take the initiative in seeking advice and support from your mentors. Schedule regular meetings or calls to discuss your progress, challenges, and plans for the future.

Show Gratitude: Express your appreciation for your mentor's time, advice, and support. A simple thank-you note or a small token of appreciation can go a long way in strengthening your relationship.

Give Back: Mentorship is a two-way street, and it's essential to contribute to the relationship by offering your support, expertise, or connections when appropriate.

Stay Connected: Maintain regular contact with your mentors, even when you don't need immediate advice or guidance. Keeping in touch through emails, phone calls, or social media can help sustain the relationship and ensure you remain on their radar.

Be Open to Feedback: Embrace constructive criticism and feedback from your mentors. Their insights can help you grow, improve, and make better decisions in your journey.

Implement Advice: Put the guidance you receive from your mentors into action. Show them that you value their input by implementing their suggestions and demonstrating your commitment to your goals.

Resources for Further Learning

As you continue to build your support network and seek mentorship, it's essential to have access to resources that can further your learning and development. Here are some suggested resources:

Books: There are numerous books on mentorship, networking, and personal growth. Some popular titles include "The Mentor's Guide" by Lois J. Zachary, "Never Eat Alone" by Keith Ferrazzi, and "How to Win Friends and Influence People" by Dale Carnegie.

Online Courses: Several online platforms offer courses on networking, communication, and personal development. Consider checking out Coursera, LinkedIn Learning, or Skillshare for relevant courses.

Podcasts: Podcasts can be a great source of inspiration and learning. Some popular podcasts on mentorship and personal development include "The Ed Mylett Show," "The Life Coach School Podcast," and "The Best One Yet."

Networking Events and Conferences: Attend industry events, conferences, and workshops to expand your network and learn from experts in your field.

Professional Organizations: Join professional organizations related to your industry or interests. These organizations often offer mentorship programs, networking opportunities, and resources for personal and professional growth.

In conclusion, seeking mentorship and guidance is an essential aspect of building a strong support network. Mentors can provide valuable insights, connections, and emotional support, helping you navigate the challenges and complexities of your journey. By surrounding yourself with positive influences, you can create an environment that fosters growth, learning, and success. Remember to be proactive, open to feedback, and express gratitude for the guidance and support you receive. Continuously strive to improve and expand your network, making the most of the resources available to you, and you'll be well on your way to achieving your goals.

Establishing a Personal Board of Advisors

As you work towards achieving your goals, having a strong support network is crucial. One powerful tool for building this network is establishing a personal board of advisors. This group of trusted individuals can provide guidance, insight, and connections, helping you navigate the challenges and opportunities that come your way. In this section, we will explore the benefits of having a personal board of advisors, how to select the right people, and tips for maximizing the value of your board.

The Benefits of a Personal Board of Advisors

A personal board of advisors can offer several advantages, including:

Diverse Perspectives: Board members come from different backgrounds and have unique experiences, providing a variety of viewpoints and insights to help you make informed decisions.

Accountability: Your board can hold you accountable to your goals, encouraging you to stay focused and disciplined in your pursuits.

Emotional Support: A personal board of advisors can provide encouragement and support during challenging times, helping you maintain your motivation and resilience.

Networking Opportunities: Board members can introduce you to valuable contacts and resources, expanding your network and opening up new opportunities.

Skill Development: Advisors can help you develop new skills and competencies, empowering you to tackle challenges and grow both personally and professionally.

Selecting the Right People for Your Personal Board of Advisors

Building a strong and effective personal board of advisors requires careful selection of the right individuals. Here are some tips for choosing your board members:

Identify Your Needs: Assess your current situation and goals to determine the skills, knowledge, and expertise you need in your advisors. This might include industry-specific knowledge, personal development insights, or access to networks and resources.

Look for Diversity: Aim for a diverse group of individuals with different backgrounds, experiences, and perspectives. This will ensure you receive well-rounded advice that considers various angles.

Seek Out Trustworthy Individuals: Choose people you can trust and who have your best interests at heart. Your personal board of advisors should be composed of individuals who genuinely care about your success and growth.

Prioritize Communication Skills: Select advisors who are effective communicators and listeners. They should be able to articulate their thoughts clearly and be open to engaging in constructive dialogue.

Consider Availability: Look for individuals who can commit to being available for regular meetings and discussions. This will ensure that you can consistently benefit from their guidance and support.

Maximizing the Value of Your Personal Board of Advisors

To get the most out of your personal board of advisors, consider the following strategies:

Set Clear Expectations: Clearly communicate your expectations to your board members regarding their roles, responsibilities, and the level of commitment required.

Establish Regular Meetings: Schedule regular meetings with your board members to discuss your progress, challenges, and goals. This will help keep you accountable and ensure you are consistently benefiting from their insights.

Foster Open Dialogue: Encourage honest and open discussions within your board. Be receptive to feedback and differing opinions, and don't be afraid to ask for help or advice.

Be Proactive: Actively seek out guidance from your board members, asking for their input on specific issues or challenges you are facing.

Show Gratitude: Express your appreciation for your board members' time, expertise, and support. This will help build strong relationships and ensure they remain committed to your success.

Practical Tools and Techniques for Your Personal Board of Advisors

To help facilitate your interactions with your personal board of advisors, consider implementing the following tools and techniques:

Meeting Agendas: Create agendas for your meetings to ensure you cover all the essential topics and make the most of your time together.

Goal Tracking: Develop a system for tracking your progress towards your goals, and share this with your board members. This will help them understand your current situation and provide relevant advice.

Decision-Making Frameworks: Use established decision-making frameworks, such as SWOT analysis or cost-benefit analysis, to structure discussions and evaluate options with your board.

Mentorship Programs: Participate in mentorship programs or events to connect with potential board members and expand your network.

Communication Platforms: Utilize communication tools, such as video conferencing, group chats, or collaborative document-sharing platforms, to facilitate communication and collaboration with your board members.

Realistic Expectations and Flexibility

As you work with your personal board of advisors, it's essential to maintain realistic expectations and remain flexible. Understand that your advisors may not always agree with one another, and it's ultimately up to you to make the final decision. Be open to revisiting and adjusting your plans as you receive new information or encounter unforeseen obstacles. Embrace change and adapt as needed, recognizing that your board is there to support you through these transitions.

Checkpoints and Reflection

Regularly assess your progress and the effectiveness of your personal board of advisors. Reflect on the value of the advice you have received and the impact it has had on your growth and progress. Use these reflections to identify areas for improvement and adjust your approach as needed.

Resources for Further Learning

To deepen your understanding of personal board of advisors and improve your skills in building and maintaining these relationships, consider exploring the following resources:

Books:

"The Start-Up of You: Adapt to the Future, Invest in Yourself, and Transform Your Career" by Reid Hoffman and Ben Casnocha

"Who's Got Your Back: The Breakthrough Program to Build Deep, Trusting Relationships That Create Success--and Won't Let You Fail" by Keith Ferrazzi

Websites:

Harvard Business Review (hbr.org): Search for articles related to mentorship, networking, and personal boards of advisors.

Forbes (forbes.com): Browse the site for relevant articles on personal development, mentorship, and networking.

Podcasts:

The Ed Mylett Show: Offers interviews with successful individuals discussing their journeys, insights, and advice.

The Life Coach School Podcast: Hosted by Brooke Castillo, this podcast covers various aspects of personal development, including building support networks and seeking mentorship.

By following the advice and strategies outlined in this section, you can build a strong personal board of advisors that will help guide you to success. Remember, the key is to surround yourself with diverse, trustworthy individuals who can offer valuable insights, hold you accountable, and provide the support you need to achieve your goals. With the right people by your side, there's no limit to what you can accomplish.

The Importance of Giving Back

In this section, we will explore the significance of giving back to others and how it can play a crucial role in building your support network. As you progress on your journey towards success, it's essential to remember that helping others and sharing your knowledge and resources can be just as valuable as receiving support. By giving back, you foster a sense of gratitude, strengthen your relationships, and contribute to the overall well-being of your community.

A Circle of Support: The Reciprocal Nature of Giving and Receiving

One of the most important aspects of giving back is understanding the reciprocal nature of the support you receive. When you invest time and effort into helping others, you create a positive environment where individuals are more likely to reciprocate and offer assistance when you need it. This circle of support not only benefits you but also contributes to the success and well-being of those around you.

Real-Life Examples of Giving Back

There are numerous ways to give back to others and support their personal and professional growth. Here are some examples of how successful individuals have made a difference in the lives of others:

Mentoring: Offer your time and expertise to mentor someone who is just starting in their career or facing challenges in their personal life. By sharing your knowledge and experiences, you can help them navigate obstacles and achieve their goals.

Volunteering: Participate in local community service projects, such as food drives, environmental cleanups, or educational programs. These activities allow you to use your skills and resources to improve the lives of others while also building connections with like-minded individuals.

Philanthropy: Support charitable organizations or causes that align with your values and passions. By donating your money, time, or resources, you can contribute to the greater good and make a lasting impact.

Sharing Knowledge: Offer your expertise by hosting workshops, giving presentations, or writing articles on topics you are knowledgeable about. By sharing your insights, you can help others learn and grow while also establishing yourself as a thought leader in your field.

Supporting Colleagues and Peers: Offer assistance to your coworkers, friends, or acquaintances when they need help or encouragement. This can be as simple as lending a listening ear or offering a word of advice.

The Benefits of Giving Back

As you engage in acts of giving back, you'll discover numerous benefits that enrich your life and contribute to your overall success. Some of these advantages include:

Enhanced Emotional Well-being: Research has shown that engaging in acts of kindness and altruism can improve your mood, reduce stress, and increase overall life satisfaction.

Stronger Relationships: By offering support to others, you create bonds of trust and respect that can lead to lasting, mutually beneficial relationships.

Increased Opportunities: Giving back can open doors to new opportunities by expanding your network, showcasing your skills, and demonstrating your commitment to your community.

Personal Growth: Helping others often presents challenges that require creative problem-solving and critical thinking. By overcoming these hurdles, you can develop essential skills and grow as a person.

Sense of Purpose: Engaging in acts of giving back can provide a sense of purpose and fulfillment, knowing that your efforts have a positive impact on others' lives.

Practical Tools and Techniques for Giving Back

To make the most of your efforts to give back, consider incorporating the following tools and techniques into your routine:

Time Management: Prioritize your time and allocate specific hours for giving back, whether it's volunteering, mentoring, or engaging in other forms of support.

Networking: Actively engage in networking events and communities where you can connect with individuals who may benefit from your support.

Skill Development: Continuously develop your skills and knowledge, so you are better equipped to provide assistance andadvice to those in need.

Collaboration: Partner with organizations, businesses, or individuals who share your values and goals. By working together, you can amplify your impact and extend your reach.

Reflection: Regularly reflect on your experiences of giving back, and assess the impact of your efforts. This can help you identify areas for improvement and guide your future actions.

Creating Checkpoints and Reflection Opportunities

To ensure that your efforts to give back remain focused and effective, it's essential to establish checkpoints and reflection opportunities. These moments can help you evaluate your progress, identify areas for growth, and maintain your motivation to continue supporting others. Consider implementing the following strategies:

Set Goals: Establish clear, measurable goals for your giving back efforts. This could include the number of hours you commit to volunteering, the number of people you mentor, or the financial contributions you make to charitable organizations.

Track Your Progress: Regularly monitor your progress towards your giving back goals. This can help you identify successes and areas where you may need to adjust your efforts.

Reflect on Your Impact: Take time to reflect on the impact your actions have had on others and your community. This can provide valuable insights into how you can continue to improve and make a difference.

Seek Feedback: Request feedback from those you've supported, as well as your peers and mentors. Their perspectives can help you understand the effectiveness of your efforts and identify areas for growth.

Celebrate Successes: Acknowledge and celebrate your achievements in giving back. This can help maintain your motivation and reinforce the importance of your efforts.

Resources for Further Learning

To deepen your understanding of the importance of giving back and enhance your ability to support others, consider exploring the following resources:

Books:

"Give and Take: Why Helping Others Drives Our Success" by Adam Grant

"The Power of One: How Ordinary People Can Make an Extraordinary Difference" by Bryce Courtenay

"The 7 Habits of Highly Effective People" by Stephen Covey

Websites:

VolunteerMatch (www.volunteermatch.org) – A platform that connects individuals with volunteer opportunities in their local communities.

Mentor: The National Mentoring Partnership (www.mentoring.org) – An organization that provides resources and support for individuals interested in becoming mentors.

Charity Navigator (www.charitynavigator.org) – A tool for researching and evaluating charitable organizations to ensure your donations have the most significant impact.

Workshops and Seminars:

Local community centers, universities, and non-profit organizations often host workshops and seminars focused on giving back and community involvement. Check their event calendars for opportunities to learn and network with like-minded individuals.

In conclusion, giving back is a vital component of building a robust support network and achieving personal and professional success. By helping others, you create a circle of support that fosters growth, strengthens relationships, and promotes overall well-being. As you embark on your journey to give back, remember to set clear goals, establish checkpoints for reflection, and continuously seek opportunities for personal growth and learning. In doing so, you will not only enrich the lives of others but also experience the profound rewards that come from contributing to the greater good.

Chapter Six

Chapter 6: Mastering Communication and Influence

Active Listening and Empathy

In a world full of distractions and constant noise, the art of active listening and empathy has become more crucial than ever. This section will explore the importance of these skills in mastering communication and influence, while providing actionable advice, practical tools, and resources for further learning.

The Power of Active Listening

Active listening is a skill that goes beyond simply hearing the words someone says. It requires being fully present and engaged, absorbing the meaning behind the words, and responding thoughtfully. Active listening helps build rapport, fosters understanding, and creates a strong foundation for effective communication.

The Benefits of Active Listening: Active listening can lead to improved relationships, increased trust, and a better understanding of others' perspectives. By actively listening, you demonstrate respect and genuine interest in the speaker, which helps create an open and supportive environment for meaningful conversations.

The Barriers to Active Listening: Common obstacles to active listening include distractions, preconceived notions, and emotional reactions. To overcome these barriers, focus on being present, setting aside judgments, and managing your emotional responses.

The Techniques of Active Listening: There are several techniques to improve your active listening skills, such as maintaining eye contact, using open body language, and summarizing or paraphrasing what the speaker said. By practicing these techniques, you can become a more attentive and effective listener.

The Role of Empathy in Communication

Empathy, the ability to understand and share another person's feelings and emotions, is a crucial component of effective communication. By practicing empathy, you can create stronger connections, resolve conflicts more effectively, and foster a supportive environment for open communication.

The Benefits of Empathy: Empathy enables you to see situations from others' perspectives, which can help you navigate difficult conversations, understand diverse viewpoints, and find common ground. Empathy also helps to create a safe space for people to express themselves openly, fostering trust and collaboration.

The Challenges of Empathy: Some common challenges to empathy include personal biases, cultural differences, and a lack of self-awareness. Overcoming these challenges requires self-reflection, a willingness to learn, and an open-minded approach to understanding others.

The Techniques for Cultivating Empathy: To develop empathy, practice active listening, ask open-ended questions, and use your imagination to put yourself in another person's shoes. By doing so, you can better understand their emotions and experiences, allowing you to communicate more effectively.

Practical Steps for Improving Active Listening and Empathy

To enhance your active listening and empathy skills, consider implementing the following strategies:

Eliminate Distractions: Create an environment that minimizes distractions, such as turning off electronic devices and choosing a quiet space for conversations. This will enable you to focus your attention fully on the speaker and listen more effectively.

Practice Mindfulness: Mindfulness techniques, such as meditation and deep breathing, can help you become more present and aware in your interactions with others. By practicing mindfulness, you can improve your ability to listen actively and empathize with others.

Engage in Role-Playing Exercises: Participate in role-playing exercises with a friend or colleague to practice active listening and empathy in a controlled setting. This can help you identify areas for improvement and develop your skills in a safe environment.

Reflect on Your Experiences: Regularly reflect on your experiences with active listening and empathy, assessing your progress and identifying areas for growth. This self-reflection can help you stay accountable and continue improving your communication skills.

Seek Feedback: Ask for feedback from friends, family, or colleagues on your active listening and empathy skills. Their input can provide valuable insights and help you identify areas for improvement.

Resources forFurther Learning

To continue developing your active listening and empathy skills, consider exploring the following resources:

Books:

a. "Just Listen: Discover the Secret to Getting Through to Absolutely Anyone" by Mark Goulston: This book offers practical advice on how to become a better listener and connect more effectively with others.

b. "Nonviolent Communication: A Language of Life" by Marshall B. Rosenberg: This book provides an in-depth look at compassionate communication techniques, including active listening and empathy.

Online Courses:

a. "Improving Communication Skills" by the University of Pennsylvania (Coursera): This online course covers various aspects of effective communication, including active listening and empathy.

b. "The Science of Well-Being" by Yale University (Coursera): This course includes a module on empathy and its role in improving well-being and communication.

Workshops and Seminars: Look for local workshops, seminars, or professional development opportunities that focus on active listening, empathy, and communication skills. These events can provide hands-on practice and valuable insights from experienced professionals.

Support Groups: Join a support group or networking organization focused on communication and personal development. These groups can offer a supportive environment to practice your skills, share experiences, and learn from others.

Podcasts and Videos: There are numerous podcasts and videos available on the topics of active listening and empathy. Some examples include "The Art of Charm" podcast, which often discusses communication skills, and TED Talks such as "The Power of Vulnerability" by Brené Brown.

By actively engaging in these resources and continually practicing your active listening and empathy skills, you can become a master of communication and influence. Remember that personal growth is a lifelong journey, and with dedication and effort, you can make significant progress in your ability to connect with others and create meaningful relationships.

Persuasive Storytelling

The ability to communicate effectively is essential in both personal and professional settings, and persuasive storytelling is a powerful tool to inspire, motivate, and influence others. By connecting with your audience through compelling stories, you can create a deep emotional impact that captures their attention, resonates with their values, and motivates them to take action.

In this section, we will explore the power of persuasive storytelling, share relatable experiences and research, offer actionable advice, and provide you with tools and techniques to master this essential skill. We will also discuss setting realistic expectations, adapting your storytelling style, and reflecting on your progress. Additionally, we will provide resources for further learning to help you continually develop your storytelling prowess.

The Science Behind Persuasive Storytelling

Numerous studies have shown that our brains are hardwired to respond to stories. When we listen to a well-told narrative, our brain releases oxytocin, a hormone that enhances empathy and trust. This, in turn, helps us to connect with the storyteller and absorb the message more effectively.

Furthermore, stories are a natural way for humans to process and retain information. They provide context and meaning, allowing us to better remember and relate to the information being shared. As a result, incorporating storytelling into your communication repertoire can significantly enhance your ability to influence and persuade others.

The Structure of a Persuasive Story

A persuasive story typically follows a three-act structure:

Setup: Introduce the characters, setting, and context. Create a relatable scenario that your audience can identify with and feel emotionally connected to.

Conflict: Present the challenges or obstacles that the characters face. This is the heart of your story, where you build tension and create a sense of urgency for your audience.

Resolution: Show how the characters overcome their challenges and achieve their goals. Offer a clear and compelling call to action, inspiring your audience to take the desired steps.

Incorporating these elements into your storytelling will help you create a captivating narrative that holds your audience's attention and drives them to take action.

The Power of Vulnerability and Authenticity

One of the most effective ways to connect with your audience is by sharing your own experiences and emotions. By being open and vulnerable, you demonstrate that you are human and relatable, which helps to build trust and rapport with your listeners.

When telling your story, be genuine and sincere. Share both your successes and your struggles, and don't be afraid to admit your mistakes or shortcomings. This authenticity will make your story more powerful and compelling, and it will encourage your audience to empathize with you and be more receptive to your message.

Using Metaphors and Analogies

Metaphors and analogies are powerful storytelling tools that can help clarify complex concepts and make abstract ideas more concrete and relatable. By drawing comparisons to familiar objects, situations, or experiences, you can help your audience better understand your message and create a lasting impression.

For example, if you're trying to convey the importance of perseverance, you might compare it to climbing a mountain. This analogy paints a vivid picture in the listener's mind, helping them grasp the concept more easily and remember it more effectively.

Tailoring Your Story to Your Audience

To maximize the impact of your story, it's essential to adapt your narrative to the needs, values, and preferences of your audience. Consider factors such as their age, culture, education, and professional background when crafting your story, and choose language, tone, and examples that will resonate with them.

By tailoring your story to your audience, you can create a stronger emotional connection and increase the likelihood that they will be receptive to your message and motivated to take action.

Practicing and Refining Your Storytelling Skills

Like any other skill, becoming a master storyteller requires practice and refinement. Dedicate time to honing your craft, experimenting with different storytelling techniques, and learning from your successes and failures.

One effective way to improve your storytelling is to seek feedback from others. Share your stories with friends, colleagues, or mentors, and ask for their honest opinions and suggestions. This constructive criticism will help you identify areas where you can improve and grow as a storyteller.

Additionally, expose yourself to a wide variety of storytelling styles and formats by attending workshops, reading books, watching TED Talks, or participating in storytelling events. This exposure will provide you with inspiration and broaden your understanding of what makes a story compelling and persuasive.

Creating Checkpoints and Reflection

As you work on improving your storytelling skills, it's important to regularly reflect on your progress and evaluate your growth. Set checkpoints for yourself where you can assess your development and identify areas where you can continue to improve.

Consider keeping a journal to document your storytelling journey, noting your successes, challenges, and lessons learned. This will help you track your progress over time and provide valuable insights into your growth as a storyteller.

Resources for Further Learning

To further develop your persuasive storytelling abilities, consider exploring the following resources:

Books:

"The Anatomy of Story" by John Truby

"Made to Stick: Why Some Ideas Survive and Others Die" by Chip Heath and Dan Heath

"Storytelling with Data: A Data Visualization Guide for Business Professionals" by Cole Nussbaumer Knaflic

Websites:

The Moth (themoth.org) - A nonprofit organization dedicated to the art of storytelling, offering live events, podcasts, and workshops.

TED Talks (ted.com) - A vast library of inspiring and informative speeches by expert storytellers, covering a wide range of topics.

Workshops and Courses:

Local storytelling workshops or meetups in your area.

Online courses and webinars focused on storytelling, public speaking, and communication skills.

In conclusion, persuasive storytelling is a powerful communication tool that can help you connect with others, inspire action, and influence decisions. By developing your storytelling skills and incorporating the strategies and techniques discussed in this section, you can become a more effective and influential communicator in both your personal and professional life. Embrace the art of storytelling, and watch as your ability to connect with and impact others flourishes.

Assertiveness and Confidence

Assertiveness is the ability to express your thoughts, feelings, and needs in an open, honest, and respectful way. It is a balanced approach to communication that avoids the extremes of passive or aggressive behavior. When you are assertive, you stand up for yourself and your rights without violating the rights of others.

Assertiveness can benefit your life in several ways:

Improved relationships: Assertive communication can help you develop more honest and open relationships, as you are better able to express your needs and listen to the needs of others.

Increased self-esteem: As you become more assertive, you gain a greater sense of self-worth and confidence in your abilities.

Reduced stress: Assertiveness can help you manage stress more effectively by allowing you to set boundaries and communicate your needs clearly.

Greater influence: Assertive individuals are often seen as more credible and persuasive, as they can express their ideas and opinions confidently and respectfully.

Building Confidence Through Communication

Confidence is a belief in your abilities and the conviction that you can achieve your goals. It is an essential quality for effective communication, as it allows you to express yourself with clarity and conviction. When you communicate with confidence, you project an air of authority and credibility that can be persuasive and influential.

Developing assertiveness and confidence is not a one-time event but a continuous process that requires practice and commitment. The following strategies can help you become more assertive and confident in your communication:

Understand your rights and values: Begin by identifying your personal rights and values. This will provide a foundation for assertive communication, as you will be better equipped to stand up for your beliefs and needs.

Practice self-awareness: Reflect on your communication style and identify any areas where you may be passive or aggressive. By being aware of your tendencies, you can work on adjusting your communication style to be more assertive.

Use "I" statements: When expressing your thoughts and feelings, use "I" statements to focus on your own experience rather than making accusations or assumptions about others. This can help reduce defensiveness and promote open communication.

Learn to say "no": Develop the ability to say "no" when necessary, without feeling guilty or apologetic. This will help you set boundaries and protect your time and energy.

Practice assertive body language: Stand tall, maintain eye contact, and use open gestures to project confidence and assertiveness.

Develop your public speaking skills: Public speaking is a powerful way to build confidence and improve your communication skills. Join a local Toastmasters club or enroll in a public speaking course to hone your abilities.

Cultivating Flexibility in Communication

While assertiveness and confidence are important communication skills, it is also crucial to be adaptable and flexible in your approach. Recognize that different situations may call for different communication styles, and be prepared to adjust your style as needed. This flexibility will allow you to navigate a variety of social and professional settings with ease and effectiveness.

Introducing Practical Exercises and Techniques

The following exercises can help you practice assertiveness and confidence in your communication:

Role-playing: Practice assertive communication with a friend or family member by role-playing various scenarios. This will help you develop your skills in a safe and supportive environment.

Visualization: Imagine yourself in a challenging situation where you need to be assertive and confident. Visualize yourself communicating effectively and standing up for your needs. This mental rehearsal can help build confidence and prepare you for real-life situations.

Assertiveness journal: Keep a journal to track your progress in becoming more assertive. Record situations where you successfully communicated assertively and those where you struggled. Reflect on your experiences and identify areas for improvement.

Positive affirmations: Develop positive affirmations related to assertiveness and confidence, such as "I am confident in my ability to express my needs" or "I deserve to be treated with respect." Repeat these affirmations daily to reinforce your belief in your abilities.

Practice self-compassion: Be kind to yourself as you develop your assertiveness and confidence. Recognize that growth takes time and that setbacks are a normal part of the process.

Creating Checkpoints and Reflection

As you work on developing your assertiveness and confidence, it is important to regularly assess your progress and reflect on your experiences. Consider setting specific goals for yourself, such as practicing assertiveness in a particular situation or increasing your confidence in public speaking. Review your goals periodically and adjust them as needed based on your progress and experiences.

Resources for Further Learning

To deepen your understanding of assertiveness and confidence and continue your personal growth, consider exploring the following resources:

Books:

"The Assertiveness Workbook" by Randy J. Paterson

"The Confidence Gap" by Russ Harris

"The Charisma Myth" by Olivia Fox Cabane

Websites and blogs:

Psychology Today (www.psychologytoday.com) - Offers articles on assertiveness, confidence, and communication skills.

Mind Tools (www.mindtools.com) - Provides resources and tools for personal and professional development, including articles on assertiveness and confidence.

Workshops and courses:

Assertiveness training workshops are often offered by local community organizations, colleges, or professional development centers.

Online platforms like Coursera and Udemy offer courses on communication skills, assertiveness, and confidence.

By committing to the development of your assertiveness and confidence, you can greatly enhance your communication skills and your ability to influence and persuade others. Embrace the journey, practice regularly, and remember that personal growth is a lifelong endeavor. As you cultivate these essential communication skills, you will find yourself better equipped to navigate the challenges and opportunities that life presents, ultimately leading to greater success and fulfillment.

Building Trust and Rapport

In the journey to mastering communication and influence, one of the most critical components is establishing trust and rapport with others. Trust is the foundation of all relationships, both personal and professional, and is essential for creating a connection that allows you to communicate effectively and influence others. Rapport is the sense of harmony and understanding that develops between people when they share a common ground or bond. When trust and rapport are established, people are more open to listening to your ideas, considering your perspective, and being influenced by your message. In this section, we will explore the importance of building trust and rapport, share actionable advice, and offer practical tools and techniques to help you improve your relationships and communication skills.

The Power of Trust and Rapport in Communication

Trust and rapport play a vital role in effective communication and influence. When people trust you, they are more likely to listen to your ideas, consider your perspective, and be open to your influence. Rapport, on the other hand, helps create a comfortable and relaxed atmosphere that fosters open and honest communication. Together, trust and rapport create a strong foundation for successful communication and influence.

Here are some benefits of building trust and rapport:

Improved collaboration: When trust and rapport are established, people are more willing to share ideas and work together towards a common goal.

Enhanced credibility: Trust and rapport enhance your credibility, making people more receptive to your message and increasing the likelihood of them taking action.

Greater empathy: When you have rapport with someone, you are more likely to understand their feelings, thoughts, and experiences, leading to more effective communication.

Reduced conflict: Trust and rapport can help diffuse tension and reduce conflict in interpersonal relationships.

Increased influence: When people trust you and feel connected to you, they are more likely to be influenced by your ideas and suggestions.

Actionable Advice for Building Trust and Rapport

Building trust and rapport takes time and effort, but the rewards are well worth it. Here are some practical steps you can take to cultivate trust and rapport in your relationships:

Be genuine: To build trust and rapport, it is essential to be genuine and authentic in your interactions with others. Be true to yourself and your values, and avoid trying to be something you are not.

Show empathy: Demonstrating empathy and understanding for others' feelings and experiences is a powerful way to build rapport. Listen actively, validate their emotions, and be supportive.

Be reliable: Consistently following through on your promises and commitments is a crucial aspect of building trust. When you are dependable, people are more likely to trust you and view you as a reliable resource.

Be open and honest: Transparency and honesty are key elements of trust. Share information openly, admit when you make mistakes, and be willing to discuss difficult topics.

Demonstrate competence: People are more likely to trust you if they believe you are competent and knowledgeable in your field. Continuously work on improving your skills and expertise to enhance your credibility.

Practical Tools and Techniques for Building Trust and Rapport

In addition to the actionable advice shared above, there are several practical tools and techniques that can help you build trust and rapport more effectively. These include:

Mirroring: Mirroring is a powerful technique that involves subtly imitating the body language, tone of voice, or speech patterns of the person you are communicating with. This can create a sense of connection and rapport, as people tend to feel more comfortable with those who are similar to them.

Active listening: Active listening involves fully focusing on the speaker, avoiding distractions, and providing feedback to show understanding. This helps build rapport by demonstrating that you value the other person's thoughts and opinions.

Open-ended questions: Asking open-ended questions that encourage deeper conversation can help build rapport by showing genuine interest in the other person's thoughts and experiences. These questions often start with "how," "what," or "why," and allow the other person to share more information about themselves.

Finding common ground: Identifying shared interests or experiences can create a sense of connection and rapport. Look for opportunities to discuss common topics or activities that both you and the other person enjoy.

Paying compliments: Genuine compliments can help build rapport by making the other person feel valued and appreciated. Be specific and sincere when offering praise or compliments.

Maintaining eye contact: Eye contact is an essential aspect of building trust and rapport. Maintaining appropriate eye contact during conversations shows that you are engaged and attentive to the other person's thoughts and feelings.

Sharing personal stories: Revealing personal anecdotes or experiences can help build trust by showing vulnerability and authenticity. Be mindful of the appropriate level of self-disclosure, depending on the relationship and context.

Creating Checkpoints and Reflection Opportunities

As you work on building trust and rapport, it's essential to periodically assess the progress and effectiveness of your efforts. Reflect on your interactions and consider the following questions:

Are my actions and behaviors consistent with my values and intentions?

Am I actively listening and demonstrating empathy in my conversations?

Do I follow through on my commitments and promises?

Am I transparent and honest in my communication?

Have I made an effort to find common ground and share personal experiences?

Use these reflection points to identify areas for improvement and make adjustments as needed to strengthen your trust and rapport-building skills.

Resources for Further Learning

Building trust and rapport is a lifelong journey, and there is always room for growth and improvement. To continue developing your skills in this area, consider exploring the following resources:

Books:

"The Trusted Advisor" by David H. Maister, Charles H. Green, and Robert M. Galford

"The Charisma Myth: How Anyone Can Master the Art and Science of Personal Magnetism" by Olivia Fox Cabane

"Influence: The Psychology of Persuasion" by Robert B. Cialdini

Online courses:

"Building Trust and Rapport" by LinkedIn Learning

"Communication Skills: Developing Trust and Rapport" by Udemy

Podcasts:

"The Trust Equation" by Trusted Advisor Associates

"The Art of Charm" by Jordan Harbinger

By investing in your communication skills and learning how to build trust and rapport, you will be well on your way to mastering communication and influence. This will not only improve your personal and professional relationships but also enhance your ability to inspire, motivate, and connect with others. Remember that trust and rapport are the foundations of influential communication, and with practice and dedication, you can strengthen these critical skills to achieve greater success in all aspects of your life.

Chapter Seven

Chapter 7: Embracing Change and Uncertainty

Developing Adaptability

Life is full of changes and uncertainties, but one thing is for sure: our ability to adapt to new circumstances is crucial for personal and professional success. In this section, we will explore how to develop adaptability and thrive in an ever-changing world. We will delve into real-life experiences, research-backed advice, and practical tools and techniques to help you enhance your adaptability skills.

The Journey to Adaptability

Adaptability is not a trait we are born with; rather, it is a skill we develop over time through experience, learning, and self-reflection. By understanding the importance of adaptability and taking proactive steps to cultivate this skill, you can become more resilient and better equipped to handle the challenges and opportunities that life presents.

Fostering a Growth Mindset

A growth mindset is the belief that our abilities and intelligence can be developed through hard work, learning, and persistence. This mindset is crucial for developing adaptability, as it encourages us to view change and uncertainty as opportunities for growth, rather than threats to our existing abilities or status quo.

To foster a growth mindset:

Embrace challenges: View obstacles and setbacks as opportunities for learning and growth, rather than as barriers to success.

Learn from criticism: Constructive feedback can help you identify areas for improvement and growth. Be open to receiving and learning from others' perspectives.

Persevere through setbacks: When faced with obstacles, remain persistent and focused on your goals. Recognize that setbacks are a natural part of the learning process.

Cultivating Emotional Intelligence

Emotional intelligence (EQ) is the ability to recognize, understand, and manage our own emotions, as well as the emotions of others. Developing a high EQ is essential for adaptability, as it enables us to navigate change and uncertainty with greater empathy, self-awareness, and resilience.

To enhance your emotional intelligence:

Practice self-awareness: Regularly reflect on your emotions, thoughts, and behaviors to gain a deeper understanding of your emotional landscape.

Develop empathy: Put yourself in others' shoes to better understand their feelings and perspectives.

Manage your emotions: Learn to recognize and regulate your emotional responses, especially in challenging or uncertain situations.

Embracing Flexibility and Openness

Flexibility and openness are key components of adaptability. Being open to new ideas and experiences, and being willing to change course when necessary, allows us to respond more effectively to the ever-changing landscape of life.

To cultivate flexibility and openness:

Let go of preconceived notions: Challenge your assumptions and be open to new ideas and perspectives.

Be willing to change course: Recognize when your current approach is not working and be prepared to adjust your plans or strategies as needed.

Stay curious: Approach new experiences and challenges with a sense of curiosity and wonder, rather than fear or resistance.

Developing Problem-Solving Skills

Effective problem-solving skills enable us to navigate change and uncertainty by identifying solutions and making informed decisions. By honing your problem-solving abilities, you will be better equipped to tackle challenges and adapt to new circumstances.

To improve your problem-solving skills:

Define the problem: Clearly articulate the issue you are facing and identify the desired outcome.

Generate possible solutions: Brainstorm multiple strategies or solutions to the problem, considering both conventional and unconventional approaches.

Evaluate and choose the best solution: Assess the pros and cons of each option and select the solution that is most likely to achieve the desired outcome.

Building Resilience

Resilience is the ability to bounce back from adversity and adapt to change. By developing resilience, we become more adept at handling uncertainty and better equipped to thrive in a constantly evolving world.

To build resilience:

Develop a strong support network: Surround yourself with people who can provide encouragement, guidance, and assistance during challenging times.

Practice self-care: Prioritize your physical, emotional, and mental well-being to ensure you have the energy and strength to face life's challenges.

Learn from past experiences: Reflect on previous difficulties and setbacks, and identify lessons learned and strategies that helped you overcome them.

Creating Checkpoints and Reflection Points

Regular self-reflection is crucial for developing adaptability, as it enables us to assess our progress, identify areas for improvement, and adjust our approach as needed. By establishing checkpoints and reflection points, we can ensure we stay on track and continue to grow and adapt throughout our journey.

To create checkpoints and reflection points:

Set clear goals: Establish specific, measurable, attainable, relevant, and time-bound (SMART) goals to help you stay focused and motivated.

Monitor your progress: Regularly assess your progress toward your goals and make adjustments as necessary.

Reflect on your experiences: Take time to reflect on your experiences, both successes and setbacks, to identify lessons learned and areas for growth.

Resources for Further Learning

To continue developing your adaptability skills and learn more about embracing change and uncertainty, consider exploring the following resources:

Books:

"Who Moved My Cheese?" by Spencer Johnson

"The Power of Now" by Eckhart Tolle

"Mindset: The New Psychology of Success" by Carol Dweck

Websites and articles:

Psychology Today: articles and resources related to adaptability, resilience, and personal growth

Harvard Business Review: articles and resources on adaptability, change management, and leadership

Workshops and courses:

Local workshops and seminars focused on personal and professional development

Online courses and webinars on adaptability, emotional intelligence, and growth mindset

By integrating these strategies and resources into your life, you will be well on your way to developing adaptability and thriving in the face of change and uncertainty. Remember, the journey to adaptability is a lifelong process, but with determination, self-reflection, and a willingness to embrace new experiences, you can cultivate the skills necessary to navigate life's challenges and seize opportunities for growth and success.

Cultivating an Innovation Mindset

In a world characterized by rapid change and uncertainty, it's more important than ever to cultivate an innovation mindset. This means embracing new ideas, staying curious, and remaining open to change. By doing so, you'll be better prepared to navigate the complexities of today's dynamic environment and capitalize on the opportunities that arise from these changes.

In this section, we'll delve into the various facets of cultivating an innovation mindset, exploring concepts such as fostering curiosity, embracing failure, and staying flexible. By the end, you'll have a deeper understanding of how to develop this essential skill and incorporate it into your everyday life.

Cultivating Curiosity: A Key Ingredient for Innovation

Curiosity is the driving force behind innovation. By constantly asking questions and seeking new knowledge, you can unlock your creative potential and generate groundbreaking ideas. To foster curiosity in your life, consider the following strategies:

Embrace a learner's mindset: Adopt the belief that you can always learn something new, regardless of your age or experience. Stay humble and open-minded, and never assume you have all the answers.

Ask questions: Challenge yourself to ask more questions, both in your personal and professional life. Inquire about the reasoning behind decisions, and explore alternative perspectives and solutions.

Explore new experiences: Seek out opportunities to try new things, visit new places, and meet new people. By broadening your horizons, you'll expose yourself to fresh ideas and inspiration.

The Power of Failure: Reframing Your Perception of Mistakes

Many people fear failure, viewing it as a sign of weakness or incompetence. However, failure is an essential part of the innovation process. By reframing your perception of mistakes and embracing the learning opportunities they provide, you can accelerate your growth and progress.

View failure as a learning opportunity: Recognize that failure is an inevitable part of the journey to success. When things don't go as planned, ask yourself what you can learn from the experience, and use this insight to inform your future decisions.

Develop resilience: Learn to bounce back from setbacks by cultivating a resilient mindset. Focus on the positives, practice self-compassion, and remember that failure is temporary.

Celebrate small wins: Recognize and celebrate your achievements, no matter how small. This will help build your confidence and motivate you to continue pushing your boundaries.

Staying Flexible: The Art of Adapting to Change

Innovation requires the ability to adapt to changing circumstances and remain open to new ideas. By staying flexible and agile, you can pivot when needed and seize opportunities that others may miss.

Embrace change: Recognize that change is a natural part of life, and try to view it as an opportunity for growth and development rather than a threat.

Develop a growth mindset: Cultivate the belief that your abilities can be developed through hard work, persistence, and dedication. This mindset will enable you to take on challenges and embrace change with greater ease.

Practice mindfulness: Engage in mindfulness exercises, such as meditation or deep breathing, to help you stay present and focused during times of change.

Building on Your Innovation Mindset: Strategies for Success

Now that we've explored the foundational elements of cultivating an innovation mindset, let's look at some actionable strategies for putting these concepts into practice:

Surround yourself with diverse perspectives: Seek out people who think differently than you do, and engage in open, respectful conversations. This will expose you to new ideas and challenge your assumptions.

Create an innovation-friendly environment: Encourage creativity and experimentation in your personal and professional life. This may involve setting aside time for brainstorming, allowing for trial and error, and celebrating innovative thinking.

Stay informed: Stay abreast of trends and developments in your industry or area of interest. By staying informed, you'll be better equipped to recognize opportunities for innovation and respond to changes in your environment.

Engage in lifelong learning: Continuously invest in your personal and professional growth by seeking out opportunities for learning and development. This may involve attending workshops, pursuing certifications, or joining professional organizations.

Reflect on your progress: Regularly assess your innovation mindset by reflecting on your experiences, successes, and challenges. Consider what you've learned, and identify areas where you can continue to grow and improve.

Resources for Further Learning

To support your journey toward cultivating an innovation mindset, consider exploring the following resources:

Books:

"The Innovator's DNA" by Clayton M. Christensen, Jeff Dyer, and Hal B. Gregersen

"The Lean Startup" by Eric Ries

"Creative Confidence" by Tom Kelley and David Kelley

TED Talks:

"The Surprising Habits of Original Thinkers" by Adam Grant

"The Power of Vulnerability" by Brené Brown

"The Puzzle of Motivation" by Dan Pink

Online Courses:

"Developing an Innovation Mindset" by Wharton School of the University of Pennsylvania (Coursera)

"Innovation and Creativity Management" by RWTH Aachen University (edX)

"Leading Change: Go Beyond Gamification with Gameful Learning" by the University of Michigan (Coursera)

Networking and Professional Organizations:

Join local meetup groups or professional organizations focused on innovation and creativity to connect with like-minded individuals and share ideas.

Workshops and Seminars:

Seek out workshops, seminars, and conferences on innovation, creativity, and change management to expand your knowledge and refine your skills.

In conclusion, cultivating an innovation mindset is essential in today's rapidly changing world. By fostering curiosity, reframing your perception of failure, and staying flexible, you can unlock your creative potential and seize the opportunities that arise from change and uncertainty. By implementing the strategies outlined in this section and utilizing the resources provided, you'll be well on your way to embracing change and uncertainty with confidence and success. So, take the first step today and begin your journey toward mastering the innovation mindset.

Navigating Difficult Transitions

Life is a series of transitions, whether it's a shift in your career, the end of a relationship, a move to a new city, or the loss of a loved one. Transitions, no matter how expected or unexpected, can be challenging and evoke a range of emotions such as fear, anxiety, sadness, and even excitement. In this section, we'll explore strategies for navigating difficult transitions with resilience and grace, offering actionable advice and practical tools to help you adapt to change and emerge stronger on the other side.

Personal Stories: Overcoming the Challenges of Change

Throughout life, we all encounter unexpected twists and turns that require us to adapt and grow. Sharing personal stories of overcoming challenges during difficult transitions can be a powerful way to inspire others and demonstrate that it's possible to find strength in the face of adversity. Here are a few examples:

After being laid off from her long-term job, Jane decided to use the opportunity to pursue her passion for writing. Despite initial struggles and self-doubt, she persisted and eventually published her first book, which became a bestseller.

Following a divorce, Mark found himself struggling to adapt to his new life as a single father. Through therapy, self-reflection, and support from friends and family, he learned to navigate his new reality and became a more involved and present father.

After losing her home in a natural disaster, Sarah discovered the importance of community and connection. She became an advocate for disaster preparedness and played an integral role in rebuilding her neighborhood.

Understanding the Stages of Transition

According to psychologist William Bridges, transitions involve three distinct stages: ending, neutral zone, and new beginning. Understanding these stages can help you navigate difficult transitions more effectively:

Ending: This stage involves letting go of the old situation, acknowledging the emotions that arise, and accepting that change is happening.

Neutral Zone: This is a period of uncertainty and confusion, where you may feel disoriented or overwhelmed. It's important to give yourself time to explore, reflect, and adjust during this stage.

New Beginning: In this stage, you embrace the new situation, develop new habits and patterns, and find a renewed sense of purpose.

Strategies for Navigating Difficult Transitions

Acknowledge your emotions: It's essential to recognize and accept the emotions that arise during a transition. Give yourself permission to feel and express your feelings, whether it's through journaling, talking to a therapist or trusted friend, or engaging in creative activities.

Seek support: Reach out to friends, family, support groups, or professional help to share your experiences and gain valuable insights from others who have gone through similar transitions.

Set realistic expectations: Remember that transitions take time, and it's normal to feel overwhelmed, uncertain, or disoriented. Be patient with yourself and recognize that it's a process.

Focus on what you can control: While you may not have control over the change itself, you can control how you respond to it. Focus on the aspects of your life that you can influence, and take small, actionable steps to move forward.

Practice self-care: Prioritize your physical, emotional, and mental well-being during a transition. This may include exercising regularly, maintaining a balanced diet, getting enough sleep, engaging in relaxation techniques, or setting aside time for hobbies and interests.

Develop new routines: Establishing new routines can help create a sense of stability and predictability during a transition. Identify healthy habits and activities that support your well-being and make them a regular part of your life.

Embrace a growth mindset: View the transition as an opportunity for personal growth and development. Seek out new experiences, learn from your challenges, and strive to become a more resilient, adaptable person.

Reflect on your values and priorities: Take the time to consider what is most important to you and how your values may have shifted during the transition. Align your actions and decisions with your core values to create a more fulfilling and purposeful life.

Set goals and create a plan: Having clear, achievable goals can help provide direction and focus during a transition. Break down your goals into smaller, manageable steps and create a plan to guide you towards success.

Stay flexible and adaptable: Recognize that change is an ongoing process, and circumstances may continue to evolve. Maintain a sense of flexibility and adaptability, allowing yourself to adjust your plans and expectations as needed.

Checkpoints and Reflection

As you navigate your way through difficult transitions, it's essential to regularly check in with yourself and reflect on your progress:

Assess your emotional well-being: How are you feeling emotionally? Are you giving yourself permission to feel and express your emotions? Are there any emotions you may be suppressing or avoiding?

Evaluate your support network: Are you reaching out for support when needed? Are there any additional resources or connections that could help you during this transition?

Review your self-care practices: Are you prioritizing your physical, emotional, and mental well-being? Are there any areas of self-care that need improvement or adjustment?

Reflect on your goals and progress: Are you making progress towards your goals? Are there any obstacles or challenges that need to be addressed? Are your goals still aligned with your values and priorities?

Resources for Further Learning

"Transitions: Making Sense of Life's Changes" by William Bridges – This book provides a comprehensive understanding of the stages of transition and offers practical strategies for navigating change.

"Who Moved My Cheese?" by Spencer Johnson – A short, allegorical tale that illustrates the importance of embracing change and adapting to new circumstances.

"The Power of Now" by Eckhart Tolle – This book emphasizes the importance of living in the present moment and offers tools for cultivating mindfulness during times of change.

"Designing Your Life: How to Build a Well-Lived, Joyful Life" by Bill Burnett and Dave Evans – This book provides a framework for designing your life, setting goals, and navigating transitions with intention and purpose.

"Option B: Facing Adversity, Building Resilience, and Finding Joy" by Sheryl Sandberg and Adam Grant – This book explores the concept of resilience and offers strategies for overcoming adversity and finding joy in the face of change.

In conclusion, navigating difficult transitions requires resilience, adaptability, and a willingness to embrace change. By acknowledging your emotions, seeking support, practicing self-care, and focusing on what you can control, you can successfully navigate challenging transitions and emerge stronger and more resilient. Remember that change is an inevitable part of life, and by cultivating a growth mindset and embracing uncertainty, you can thrive and flourish, even in the face of adversity.

Staying Grounded in the Present Moment

In a world filled with constant change and uncertainty, it's crucial to develop the ability to stay grounded in the present moment. By doing so, you can reduce stress, improve focus, and cultivate a more balanced and fulfilling life. In this section, we'll explore why staying present is essential, and how you can develop this essential skill.

The Power of Presence

The present moment is the only moment we truly have. The past has already happened, and the future is yet to come. When we focus on the present, we harness our full potential to create, learn, and grow. By being present, we can:

Reduce stress and anxiety: Focusing on the present moment helps us let go of worries about the future or regrets from the past, reducing stress and anxiety levels.

Improve focus and productivity: When we are fully present, we can concentrate on the task at hand, leading to higher levels of productivity and performance.

Enhance relationships: Being present allows us to truly connect with others, fostering deeper and more meaningful relationships.

Cultivate gratitude and happiness: Staying present enables us to appreciate the beauty and abundance in our lives, promoting a greater sense of happiness and well-being.

Practical Techniques for Staying Present

Developing the ability to stay grounded in the present moment is a skill that can be cultivated with practice. Here are some practical techniques you can use to enhance your presence:

Mindfulness meditation: One of the most effective ways to cultivate presence is through mindfulness meditation. This practice involves focusing your attention on your breath, bodily sensations, or a specific object or mantra, and gently bringing your attention back to the present whenever your mind wanders. Regular mindfulness meditation practice has been shown to reduce stress, improve focus, and increase emotional resilience.

Deep breathing exercises: Deep, slow breathing can help calm the mind and bring you back to the present moment. When you feel your thoughts drifting to the past or future, pause and take several deep, slow breaths, focusing on the sensation of the air entering and leaving your body.

Body scan: A body scan involves systematically focusing your attention on different parts of your body, noticing any sensations or tension you may be holding. This practice helps you become more aware of your physical presence and anchors you in the present moment.

Engage your senses: Paying attention to your senses can help you become more present. Try to notice the sounds, smells, and textures around you, as well as the taste of your food and the sensation of your breath.

Practice active listening: When engaging in conversation, make a conscious effort to listen attentively and fully, without interrupting or mentally preparing your response. This practice can help you become more present and deepen your connections with others.

Develop a present moment reminder: Choose a regular activity or object in your environment as a cue to bring your attention back to the present moment. For example, you might decide that every time you walk through a doorway, you will take a deep breath and focus on your surroundings.

Incorporate mindfulness into everyday activities: You can practice being present in your daily life by bringing mindful awareness to mundane activities, such as washing dishes, brushing your teeth, or walking. Focus on the sensations, movements, and sounds associated with each activity.

Establishing Realistic Expectations and Flexibility

Developing presence is a gradual process that requires patience and commitment. It's important to:

Be patient with yourself: Recognize that staying present is a skill that takes time and practice to develop. Be patient with yourself as you work to cultivate this ability.

Accept imperfection:

Acknowledge that you won't always be able to maintain perfect presence, and that's okay. Embrace your imperfections and remember that progress, not perfection, is the goal.

Stay flexible: Be open to trying different techniques and approaches to staying present. What works for one person may not work for another, so experiment to find what resonates with you.

Creating Checkpoints and Reflection Opportunities

Regularly reflecting on your progress and experiences can help you stay committed to cultivating presence. Consider incorporating the following practices into your routine:

Set aside time for reflection: Dedicate a specific time each day or week to reflect on your experiences with staying present. This could involve journaling, meditating, or engaging in a mindful conversation with a trusted friend or mentor.

Track your progress: Use a journal or an app to record your experiences and progress in staying present. This can help you identify patterns, recognize areas for improvement, and celebrate your successes.

Set realistic goals: Establish specific, achievable goals for enhancing your presence, such as practicing mindfulness meditation for 10 minutes a day or incorporating a daily body scan into your routine.

Resources for Further Learning

To deepen your understanding of staying grounded in the present moment and continue developing this skill, consider exploring the following resources:

Books:

"The Power of Now" by Eckhart Tolle

"Wherever You Go, There You Are" by Jon Kabat-Zinn

"The Miracle of Mindfulness" by Thich Nhat Hanh

Online courses and workshops:

Mindfulness-Based Stress Reduction (MBSR) courses, available through various institutions and online platforms

The Greater Good Science Center at UC Berkeley offers a variety of online courses on mindfulness and other topics related to well-being.

Apps:

Headspace

Calm

Insight Timer

Websites and blogs:

Mindful.org

Tiny Buddha

The Greater Good Science Center

By embracing change and uncertainty and learning to stay grounded in the present moment, you'll be better equipped to navigate the challenges and opportunities life has to offer. Remember, cultivating presence is a lifelong journey, and each step you take brings you closer to a more balanced, fulfilled, and resilient life.

Chapter Eight

Chapter 8: Personal Branding and Visibility

Crafting Your Personal Brand Story

Your personal brand story is the narrative you create to showcase your unique blend of skills, experience, and values to the world. It's the story that helps others understand who you are, what you stand for, and how you can make a difference. Crafting a compelling personal brand story is essential for gaining visibility and establishing your authority in your field. In this section, we will explore the process of developing your personal brand story, offering relatable experiences, well-researched information, actionable advice, and practical tools to help you create a strong personal brand.

Discovering Your Core Values and Passions

The foundation of your personal brand story is built upon your core values and passions. These are the guiding principles that influence your decisions, actions, and overall approach to life. To uncover your core values and passions, consider the following:

Reflect on your past experiences: Think about your life experiences, both positive and negative, and identify the moments when you felt most fulfilled, proud, or passionate. What values were you upholding during these moments? How do these experiences connect to your passions?

Identify your strengths: Recognize your unique skills, talents, and abilities that set you apart from others. These strengths will be crucial to crafting a personal brand story that highlights your distinctive qualities.

Consider your purpose: Reflect on what drives you and the impact you want to make in the world. Your purpose is the "why" behind your personal brand story and should connect to your values and passions.

Creating a Compelling Narrative

Now that you have a better understanding of your core values, passions, and strengths, it's time to weave these elements into a captivating narrative. Consider the following tips:

Be authentic: Your personal brand story should be genuine and resonate with who you are as a person. Avoid exaggerating or downplaying your experiences, as this could damage your credibility and leave a negative impression on your audience.

Share your journey: Don't be afraid to share your personal and professional experiences, including challenges and setbacks. These stories humanize your brand, making it more relatable and inspiring to others.

Showcase your unique value proposition: Clearly articulate what sets you apart from others in your field and the specific value you bring to the table. This could include unique skills, expertise, or a novel approach to problem-solving.

Putting Your Personal Brand Story into Action

Once you have crafted your personal brand story, the next step is to strategically share it with the world. Here are some practical ways to do so:

Develop your elevator pitch: Create a concise, compelling summary of your personal brand story that you can share in networking situations, interviews, or casual conversations.

Create a personal website or blog: Showcase your personal brand story, portfolio, and thought leadership on a personal website or blog. This serves as a central hub for your online presence and helps potential employers or clients learn more about you.

Leverage social media: Use social media platforms such as LinkedIn, Twitter, and Facebook to share your personal brand story and engage with your target audience. Be consistent in your messaging and ensure your online presence aligns with your personal brand story.

Network strategically: Attend industry events, conferences, and workshops to connect with like-minded professionals and share your personal brand story in person. Establishing strong relationships can open doors to new opportunities and collaborations.

Reflecting on Your Personal Brand Story

As you progress in your career and personal life, it's essential to periodically reflect on your personal brand story and make adjustments as needed. Consider the following checkpoints:

Revisit your core values and passions: Ensure your personal brand story still aligns with your values and passions, as these may evolve over time.

Assess your strengths and unique value proposition: As you gain new skills, experiences, and expertise, evaluate whether your unique value proposition needs to be updated or refined.

Review your personal and professional goals: Reflect on your current goals and aspirations and ensure that your personal brand story supports your desired trajectory.

Seek feedback from trusted peers or mentors: Ask for input from those who know you well and can provide constructive feedback on how your personal brand story resonates with others.

Evaluate your online presence: Regularly review your online presence to ensure it remains consistent with your personal brand story and up to date with your latest achievements, insights, and experiences.

Resources for Further Learning

As you work on crafting your personal brand story, it's essential to continue learning and refining your approach. Here are some resources that can help you on your journey:

Books:

"Reinventing You: Define Your Brand, Imagine Your Future" by Dorie Clark

"Crush It!: Why NOW Is the Time to Cash In on Your Passion" by Gary Vaynerchuk

"The Brand Called You: Create a Personal Brand That Wins Attention and Grows Your Business" by Peter Montoya and Tim Vandehey

Websites and Blogs:

Personal Branding Blog (https://www.personalbrandingblog.com/)

The Muse (https://www.themuse.com/)

LinkedIn Learning (https://www.linkedin.com/learning/)

Podcasts:

"The Personal Branding Podcast" by Chris Ducker

"The Life Coach School Podcast" by Brooke Castillo

"The Smart Passive Income Podcast" by Pat Flynn

By following the advice and implementing the practical tools provided in this section, you can craft a compelling personal brand story that sets you apart from the competition and attracts new opportunities. Remember to stay authentic, consistently evaluate your personal brand story, and be proactive in sharing your unique narrative with the world. With dedication and persistence, your personal brand story will become a powerful tool in propelling you towards your goals and aspirations.

Building an Online Presence

In today's digitally connected world, building an online presence is essential for personal branding and visibility. A strong online presence allows you to showcase your expertise, connect with others, and open doors to new opportunities. In this section, we will explore the key components of building an effective online presence, as well as offer practical advice and resources for further learning.

Laying the Foundation: Establishing a Consistent Online Identity

The first step in building an online presence is to establish a consistent online identity. This involves creating cohesive and recognizable branding across various digital platforms, including social media, websites, and blogs.

Choose a professional username: Your username should be consistent across all platforms and represent your personal brand. Ideally, it should be your full name or a variation thereof.

Create a high-quality profile picture: Invest in a professional headshot that reflects your personal brand and can be used consistently across all your online profiles.

Develop a compelling bio: Craft a concise and engaging bio that highlights your unique value proposition, expertise, and accomplishments. Tailor your bio for each platform, but ensure it remains consistent with your overall personal brand story.

Use a consistent design and color scheme: Apply a cohesive visual design across all your online profiles, including a consistent color scheme and typography. This will help reinforce your personal brand and make your online presence more memorable.

Expanding Your Reach: Leveraging Social Media Platforms

Social media platforms are invaluable tools for building your online presence and connecting with others in your industry. Here's how you can make the most of popular social media platforms:

LinkedIn: As a professional networking site, LinkedIn is essential for showcasing your expertise, accomplishments, and connections. Optimize your profile with a strong headline, detailed work experience, and relevant skills. Regularly share insightful content, engage with others, and build your network.

Twitter: Twitter is an excellent platform for sharing bite-sized insights, news, and updates related to your industry. Follow thought leaders, participate in relevant conversations, and use hashtags strategically to increase your visibility.

Facebook: Create a professional Facebook page separate from your personal profile. Share industry news, blog posts, and personal updates related to your personal brand. Engage with your audience through comments and direct messages.

Instagram: Use Instagram to share a more personal side of your personal brand through visuals. Post photos and stories that showcase your work, passions, and interests. Use hashtags and location tags strategically to increase your visibility.

Niche platforms: Depending on your industry, you may also want to explore niche social media platforms, such as Behance for designers, GitHub for developers, or ResearchGate for academics.

Developing Content: Sharing Your Expertise and Insights

Creating and sharing valuable content is critical for building your online presence and establishing yourself as an expert in your field. Consider the following tips for developing and sharing content:

Start a blog: A personal blog is an excellent platform for sharing your expertise, experiences, and insights. Regularly publish high-quality, long-form content that is relevant to your industry and personal brand.

Guest post on reputable websites: Submit guest posts to industry-specific websites, blogs, or online publications. This will help expand your reach, build your credibility, and drive traffic back to your own blog or website.

Share insightful content on social media: Regularly share relevant articles, news, and updates on your social media profiles. Engage with your audience by asking questions, responding to comments, and participating in discussions.

Create multimedia content: Explore different formats for sharing your expertise, such as podcasting, video creation, or webinars. This can help you reach a wider audience and cater to different learning preferences.

Collaborate with other experts: Partner with other thought leaders or influencers in your industry to create collaborative content, such as co-authored articles, joint webinars, or podcast interviews. This can help expand your reach, introduce you to new audiences, and provide fresh perspectives.

Building Credibility: Demonstrating Your Expertise and Accomplishments

Establishing credibility is crucial for building trust with your audience and positioning yourself as an authority in your field. Here are some ways to demonstrate your expertise and accomplishments:

Showcase your portfolio: Create an online portfolio to display your work, case studies, or projects. This can be part of your personal website or on a dedicated platform like Behance or Dribbble.

Highlight your achievements: Include a list of your most significant accomplishments, such as awards, publications, or speaking engagements, on your website or LinkedIn profile.

Share testimonials and endorsements: Reach out to clients, colleagues, or mentors for testimonials or endorsements that highlight your skills, work ethic, or achievements. Feature these prominently on your website or social media profiles.

Participate in industry events: Attend conferences, workshops, or networking events in your field to build connections, learn from others, and share your insights. Consider applying to speak at events or hosting your own workshops to further demonstrate your expertise.

Obtain certifications or credentials: Pursue relevant certifications, credentials, or continuing education opportunities to stay current in your industry and demonstrate your commitment to professional growth.

Monitoring Your Online Reputation: Managing Your Digital Footprint

Your online reputation plays a crucial role in your personal brand and visibility. Be proactive in monitoring and managing your digital footprint:

Set up Google Alerts: Set up Google Alerts for your name and relevant keywords to monitor mentions of your personal brand and stay informed about your online presence.

Regularly audit your online presence: Periodically review your social media profiles, blog posts, and online comments to ensure they align with your personal brand and remove or update any outdated or inappropriate content.

Respond to feedback and criticism: Engage with your audience and address any negative feedback or criticism in a professional and constructive manner.

Protect your privacy: Be mindful of the personal information you share online and adjust your privacy settings on social media platforms as necessary.

Use reputation management tools: Consider using reputation management tools, such as BrandYourself or Reputation.com, to help you monitor and improve your online presence.

Additional Resources for Further Learning

To further enhance your personal branding and visibility efforts, explore the following resources:

Books:

"Crushing It!: How Great Entrepreneurs Build Their Business and Influence-and How You Can, Too" by Gary Vaynerchuk

"Reinventing You: Define Your Brand, Imagine Your Future" by Dorie Clark

"KNOWN: The Handbook for Building and Unleashing Your Personal Brand in the Digital Age" by Mark Schaefer

Online courses:

"Personal Branding: Crafting Your Social Media Presence" on LinkedIn Learning

"The Complete Personal Branding Course" on Udemy

"How to Build a Powerful Personal Brand" on Skillshare

Blogs and websites:

WHO THE F*CK TOLD YOU IT WOULD BE EASY

Personal Branding Blog (https://www.personalbrandingblog.com/)

Branding Magazine (https://www.brandingmag.com/)

Fast Company's Leadership section (https://www.fastcompany.com/leadership)

In conclusion, building an effective online presence is essential for personal branding and visibility. By establishing a consistent online identity, leveraging social media platforms, creating valuable content, demonstrating your expertise, and managing your digital footprint, you can elevate your personal brand and open doors to new opportunities.

Networking and Relationship Building

An essential part of personal branding and visibility is effective networking and relationship building. Your connections can lead to new opportunities, collaborations, and growth, both personally and professionally. In this section, we will explore strategies and techniques to help you create and maintain meaningful relationships in your network.

The Art of Making Connections: Building Your Professional Network

To build a strong professional network, consider the following strategies:

Identify your goals: Before diving into networking, take a moment to reflect on your goals. Are you looking to expand your professional circle, find a mentor, or explore new career opportunities? Having clear objectives will help you approach networking with purpose and focus.

Attend industry events: Participate in conferences, workshops, or networking events in your field to connect with like-minded professionals. These events provide excellent opportunities to learn from others, share your insights, and expand your network.

Leverage social media: Social media platforms like LinkedIn, Twitter, and Facebook can be powerful tools for networking. Engage with others by sharing valuable content, commenting on posts, and joining relevant groups or discussions.

Build relationships, not just connections: Focus on building genuine relationships rather than merely collecting contacts. Seek to understand the needs, interests, and goals of those in your network and look for opportunities to support and collaborate.

Be proactive: Don't wait for networking opportunities to come to you. Reach out to people you admire, ask for introductions, or attend events that will put you in contact with others in your industry.

Foster a give-and-take mentality: When networking, approach each interaction with the intent to give as much as you receive. Offer your expertise, insights, or support and be open to learning from others.

Mastering the Art of Conversation: Building Rapport and Trust

Effective communication is critical to building strong relationships. Here are some tips to help you master the art of conversation and build rapport and trust with others:

Be genuinely curious: Show genuine interest in others by asking open-ended questions and listening attentively to their responses. This will help you uncover shared interests and create deeper connections.

Practice active listening: To build rapport, focus on truly understanding the other person's perspective. Practice active listening by nodding, summarizing their points, and asking follow-up questions.

Share your experiences and insights: While it's essential to listen and be curious, don't forget to share your experiences, knowledge, and insights. This can help establish your credibility and expertise in your field.

Be empathetic: Show empathy by acknowledging others' feelings and experiences. This can help create a deeper connection and build trust.

Be mindful of body language: Non-verbal cues play a significant role in communication. Maintain eye contact, use open body language, and avoid crossing your arms or checking your phone during conversations.

Be adaptable: Adjust your communication style based on the person you are speaking with and the context of the conversation. Be aware of cultural differences, preferences, and social cues.

The Power of Mentorship: Finding and Cultivating Mentors

Mentors can provide invaluable guidance, support, and inspiration as you navigate your personal and professional journey. To find and cultivate mentor relationships, consider the following:

Identify potential mentors: Look for people in your industry or field who possess the skills, knowledge, and experience you admire. This could be someone within your organization, a speaker at an event, or even an author you admire.

Approach with a clear purpose: When reaching out to potential mentors, be clear about your intentions and what you hope to gain from the relationship. Explain why you believe they would be an excellent mentor for you and what you hope to learn from them.

Be respectful of their time: Understand that mentors are often busy individuals. Be respectful of their time by being punctual, prepared, and focused during your interactions.

Maintain open communication: Keep lines of communication open and be receptive to feedback, advice, and guidance. Share updates on your progress, challenges, and successes with your mentor.

Show gratitude and appreciation: Express your appreciation for your mentor's time, support, and insights. Recognize their contributions to your growth and development.

Foster a reciprocal relationship: Mentoring relationships should be mutually beneficial. Look for opportunities to provide value to your mentor, such as sharing relevant articles, insights, or helping them with a project.

Creating a Personal Board of Advisors: Diversifying Your Support Network

In addition to cultivating mentor relationships, consider creating a personal board of advisors. This group can provide diverse perspectives, expertise, and support as you navigate your personal and professional journey. To create a personal board of advisors, consider the following:

Identify potential advisors: Look for individuals who possess different skills, backgrounds, and experiences. Aim for a diverse group that can offer varied perspectives and insights.

Set expectations: Be clear about your goals and what you hope to gain from your relationships with your advisors. Share your objectives and how you envision their role in your support network.

Communicate regularly: Maintain open lines of communication with your advisors. Schedule regular check-ins or meetings to share updates, challenges, and successes.

Be open to feedback: Be receptive to feedback and advice from your advisors, even if it may be difficult to hear. Their diverse perspectives can provide valuable insights and help you make more informed decisions.

Express gratitude: Show appreciation for your advisors' time, support, and expertise. Recognize their contributions to your growth and development.

Provide value: Look for ways to offer value to your advisors, such as sharing your expertise, resources, or connections.

Resources for Further Learning

To further develop your networking and relationship-building skills, consider exploring the following resources:

Books:

"Never Eat Alone" by Keith Ferrazzi

"How to Win Friends and Influence People" by Dale Carnegie

"The Charisma Myth" by Olivia Fox Cabane

Websites:

LinkedIn Learning: Offers numerous courses on networking, communication, and personal branding.

Harvard Business Review: Provides articles and resources on networking, relationship building, and personal growth.

Podcasts:

The Art of Charm: Offers insights and interviews on networking, communication, and social dynamics.

The Introvert's Edge: Focuses on networking and relationship-building strategies for introverts.

By integrating these strategies and techniques into your networking and relationship-building efforts, you can create a robust support network that fosters personal and professional growth. Embrace the power of connections and watch your personal brand and visibility soar.

Embracing Public Speaking and Thought Leadership

In today's rapidly evolving world, becoming a thought leader and effectively communicating your ideas can significantly boost your personal brand and visibility. Public speaking and thought leadership are powerful tools that can open doors, create connections, and influence others. In this section, we will explore the art of public speaking, the journey to becoming a thought leader, and the resources to help you excel in these areas.

Unlocking the Power of Public Speaking

Public speaking is a critical skill that can set you apart and establish your authority in your field. To excel as a public speaker, consider the following strategies:

Overcoming the fear of public speaking: Fear of public speaking is common, but with practice and the right mindset, you can overcome it. Embrace vulnerability, focus on the value you bring to your audience, and practice deep breathing techniques to calm your nerves.

Knowing your audience: Understand your audience's needs, interests, and expectations. Tailor your message to resonate with them and provide valuable insights.

Structuring your talk: Create a clear structure for your speech, with an engaging introduction, a compelling body, and a memorable conclusion. Use stories, anecdotes, and examples to illustrate your points and maintain audience interest.

Mastering non-verbal communication: Your body language, facial expressions, and gestures convey as much information as your words. Practice effective non-verbal communication techniques to create a strong presence and connection with your audience.

Enhancing your vocal variety: Vary your pitch, volume, and pace to create an engaging and dynamic speaking style. Use pauses strategically to emphasize key points and allow your audience to digest your message.

Inviting audience interaction: Encourage audience participation through questions, discussions, and activities. Engaging your audience makes your talk more memorable and impactful.

Receiving and implementing feedback: Solicit feedback from trusted peers, mentors, or coaches to identify areas for improvement. Implement the feedback to refine and elevate your public speaking skills.

Embracing Thought Leadership

Becoming a thought leader allows you to share your expertise, inspire others, and create meaningful change in your field. The journey to thought leadership involves the following steps:

Identifying your niche: Determine the specific area in which you want to establish yourself as a thought leader. Choose a topic that aligns with your passion, expertise, and the needs of your target audience.

Developing your unique perspective: Cultivate a unique point of view and approach to your chosen niche. Embrace your personal experiences, insights, and beliefs to distinguish yourself from others in your field.

Creating valuable content: Share your expertise through articles, blogs, videos, podcasts, and social media posts. Provide actionable advice, thought-provoking insights, and valuable resources to help your audience grow and succeed.

Engaging with your audience: Respond to comments, questions, and messages from your audience. Engage in discussions, debates, and collaborations to foster connections and build your community.

Participating in industry events: Attend conferences, seminars, and workshops in your field to expand your network, learn from others, and share your expertise.

Continuously learning and growing: Stay informed about the latest trends, research, and developments in your field. Embrace lifelong learning to ensure your thought leadership remains relevant and impactful.

Practical Tools and Techniques to Enhance Your Public Speaking and Thought Leadership

Visualization: Imagine yourself delivering a successful talk or presentation. Envision the audience's positive reactions, your confidence, and the impact of your message.

Power poses: Adopt powerful and confident body language before your talk to boost your self-esteem and energy levels.

Breathing exercises: Practice deep breathing techniques to calm your nerves and focus your mind before and during your talk.

Video recording: Record your speeches or presentations and review them to identify areas for improvement. Observe your body language, vocal variety, and audience engagement.

Join a public speaking group: Participate in organizations like Toastmasters International to improve your public speaking skills in a supportive and structured environment.

Attend workshops and courses: Invest in your personal development by attending workshops, courses, and training programs on public speaking and thought leadership.

Collaborate with mentors or coaches: Seek guidance from experienced public speakers, thought leaders, or coaches to accelerate your learning and growth.

Realistic Expectations and Flexibility

Embracing public speaking and thought leadership is a journey that requires patience, persistence, and a growth mindset. Set realistic expectations and be prepared to adapt and evolve as you learn and grow. Celebrate your progress, learn from setbacks, and maintain a positive attitude throughout your journey.

Checkpoints and Reflection

Regularly assess your progress and reflect on your experiences as a public speaker and thought leader. Identify areas for improvement, celebrate your successes, and adjust your approach as needed.

Resources for Further Learning

Books:

"Talk Like TED" by Carmine Gallo

"The Art of Public Speaking" by Dale Carnegie and J. Berg Esenwein

"Thought Leadership: Prompting Businesses to Think and Learn" by Mindy Gibbins-Klein

Websites:

Toastmasters International (www.toastmasters.org)

TED Talks (www.ted.com)

Harvard Business Review (www.hbr.org)

Online courses:

Coursera: "Introduction to Public Speaking"

LinkedIn Learning: "Becoming a Thought Leader"

MasterClass: "Chris Anderson Teaches Public Speaking"

In conclusion, embracing public speaking and thought leadership can significantly enhance your personal brand and visibility. By cultivating your public speaking skills, developing a unique perspective, and engaging with your audience, you can inspire others, create meaningful connections, and become an influential voice in your field. Invest in your personal growth, seek guidance from mentors and coaches, and leverage the wealth of resources available to help you excel on your journey. With persistence and a growth mindset, you can achieve success as a public speaker and thought leader.

Chapter Nine

Chapter 9: Achieving Work-Life Balance

Defining Your Personal Values

Achieving a work-life balance is a challenge faced by many people in today's fast-paced world. In order to find this balance, it is essential to define your personal values, as they will guide your decisions and actions throughout your life. By understanding and prioritizing your values, you can create a fulfilling life that aligns with your deepest beliefs and desires.

In this section, we will explore the importance of personal values, provide practical tools to identify and prioritize your values, and share strategies to integrate these values into your daily life. This will enable you to create a foundation for achieving work-life balance and living a life that is true to yourself.

The Importance of Personal Values

Personal values are the guiding principles that define what is truly important to you. They shape your beliefs, attitudes, and behaviors, influencing your decision-making process and how you prioritize your time and resources. When your actions align with your values, you experience greater satisfaction, fulfillment, and well-being.

Some benefits of identifying and living in accordance with your personal values include:

Enhanced self-awareness: Understanding your values enables you to develop a deeper understanding of your true self, providing clarity and direction in your life.

Improved decision-making: When you are aware of your values, you can make decisions that are more aligned with your core beliefs, leading to greater satisfaction and reduced stress.

Increased motivation and productivity: Aligning your work and personal life with your values can enhance your motivation and productivity, as you are more likely to be engaged in activities that are meaningful and fulfilling.

Stronger relationships: When you understand your values and those of others, you can build stronger and more authentic relationships based on shared values and mutual respect.

Greater resilience: Living in alignment with your values can provide a strong foundation for coping with challenges and adversity, as you are more likely to persevere when your actions are driven by deeply-held beliefs.

Identifying and Prioritizing Your Personal Values

In order to align your life with your values, you must first identify and prioritize them. The following steps can help you in this process:

Brainstorm a list of values: Begin by creating a list of values that resonate with you. Consider aspects of your life that are most important, such as family, career, health, spirituality, or personal growth. You may also draw inspiration from role models, books, or other sources of inspiration.

Narrow down your list: Review your list and eliminate any values that are less important or redundant. Aim to identify the top 10-15 values that are most significant to you.

Prioritize your values: Rank your values in order of importance, from most to least important. This will help you focus on the values that are most essential to your well-being and happiness.

Reflect on your current alignment: Consider how well your current actions and decisions align with your prioritized values. Identify any areas where there may be misalignment or room for improvement.

Create an action plan: Develop a plan to align your life more closely with your values. Set specific goals and identify concrete steps you can take to achieve these goals, such as adjusting your work schedule, spending more time with loved ones, or pursuing personal development opportunities.

Integrating Personal Values into Your Daily Life

Once you have identified and prioritized your personal values, the next step is to integrate them into your daily life. The following strategies can help you live in alignment with your values and create a more balanced and fulfilling life:

Set value-based goals: Set goals that are aligned with your personal values, and break them down into smaller, actionable steps. This can help ensure that your actions are consistent with your beliefs and priorities, leading to a more balanced and fulfilling life.

Establish routines and habits: Create routines and habits that support your values and help you maintain work-life balance. For example, if health is a priority, incorporate regular exercise and healthy eating habits into your daily routine. If family is important, establish routines for quality time with your loved ones.

Be mindful of your values in decision-making: When faced with decisions, consider how each option aligns with your values. Make choices that support your values and contribute to a balanced and fulfilling life.

Develop resilience: Embrace the challenges and setbacks that arise as you strive to live in alignment with your values. Learn from these experiences and use them to strengthen your commitment to your values and your overall well-being.

Seek support: Surround yourself with people who share your values and can provide encouragement, guidance, and support as you work towards achieving work-life balance.

Review and reassess: Periodically review your values and assess how well you are living in alignment with them. Adjust your goals and strategies as needed to maintain balance and prioritize what is most important to you.

Be flexible and adaptive: Recognize that your values may evolve over time as you grow and encounter new experiences. Be open to reevaluating and adjusting your values as needed to continue living a fulfilling and balanced life.

Resources for Further Learning

To deepen your understanding of personal values and their role in achieving work life balance, consider exploring the following resources:

Books:

"The 7 Habits of Highly Effective People" by Stephen Covey

"Dare to Lead" by Brené Brown

"Man's Search for Meaning" by Viktor Frankl

Websites:

The Values in Action (VIA) Institute on Character (www.viacharacter.org) – Offers resources and assessments to help you identify and develop your character strengths and values.

MindTools (www.mindtools.com) – Provides tools, resources, and articles on various aspects of personal and professional development, including values and work-life balance.

Podcasts:

"The Life Coach School Podcast" with Brooke Castillo – Offers advice on personal development, goal setting, and living a values-based life.

"The Best One Yet" with Michael Hyatt – Focuses on personal and professional growth, including topics such as values, goal setting, and work-life balance.

In conclusion, defining your personal values is a critical step in achieving work-life balance. By identifying and prioritizing your values, you can make more informed decisions, set meaningful goals, and create a life that aligns with your core beliefs. By integrating your values into your daily life, you will experience greater satisfaction, fulfillment, and well-being, ultimately leading to a more balanced and purposeful life.

Setting Boundaries and Managing Stress

Establishing boundaries is crucial for maintaining a healthy work-life balance. Boundaries help you create space for personal growth, self-care, and nurturing relationships, while also protecting your time, energy, and well-being. Setting boundaries can involve establishing limits on work hours, screen time, or social interactions and ensuring that you have dedicated time for self-care and relaxation.

Tips for Setting Boundaries

Identify your priorities: Determine the most important aspects of your life, such as family, career, health, and personal development. Create boundaries that protect and prioritize these areas.

Communicate your boundaries: Clearly communicate your boundaries to others, such as family members, friends, and colleagues. Be assertive but respectful when discussing your boundaries, and be open to feedback and negotiation.

Be consistent: Consistently enforce your boundaries, even when faced with pressure or resistance from others. This will help you maintain a sense of control and balance in your life.

Practice self-awareness: Pay attention to your thoughts, feelings, and physical sensations when your boundaries are being tested. This will help you recognize when you need to assert yourself and protect your boundaries.

Allow for flexibility: While it's important to be consistent with your boundaries, also recognize that life can be unpredictable, and sometimes flexibility is necessary. Be open to adjusting your boundaries as needed but maintain a focus on your priorities.

Managing Stress and Integrating Self-Care Practices

Stress is an inevitable part of life, but it is essential to manage it effectively to maintain a healthy work-life balance. Incorporating self-care practices and stress-management techniques can help you prevent burnout and maintain a sense of well-being.

Tips for Managing Stress and Integrating Self-Care Practices

Develop a self-care routine: Identify activities that help you relax, recharge, and maintain your well-being. Incorporate these activities into your daily or weekly routine.

Prioritize sleep: Ensure that you get enough rest to help manage stress and maintain overall health. Establish a bedtime routine, maintain a consistent sleep schedule, and create a comfortable sleep environment.

Exercise regularly: Engage in regular physical activity to help reduce stress, improve mood, and maintain overall health. Find an exercise routine that you enjoy and can commit to consistently.

Cultivate mindfulness: Practice mindfulness techniques, such as meditation or deep breathing exercises, to help manage stress and increase self-awareness.

Connect with others: Nurture relationships with friends and family members who support and understand your need for balance. Seek out social support and share your experiences with others.

Seek professional help: If you are struggling to manage stress or maintain work-life balance, consider seeking professional help from a therapist, counselor, or life coach.

Checkpoints and Reflection

As you work on setting boundaries and managing stress, it is essential to periodically reflect on your progress and make adjustments as needed. Consider the following questions to assess your progress and identify areas for improvement:

Are my boundaries helping me maintain a healthy work-life balance?

Am I effectively managing stress and incorporating self-care practices into my daily routine?

Do I need to make any adjustments to my boundaries or stress-management strategies to maintain balance and well-being?

Resources for Further Learning

To deepen your understanding of setting boundaries and managing stress, consider exploring the following resources:

Books:

"Boundaries: When to Say Yes, How to Say No

To Take Control of Your Life" by Dr. Henry Cloud and Dr. John Townsend

"The Stress-Proof Brain: Master Your Emotional Response to Stress Using Mindfulness and Neuroplasticity" by Dr. Melanie Greenberg

"Burnout: The Secret to Unlocking the Stress Cycle" by Emily Nagoski and Amelia Nagoski

Websites and online resources:

TED Talks on work-life balance and stress management: Visit the TED website to explore a variety of talks discussing the importance of work-life balance and stress management.

Mindful.org: This website offers articles, guided meditations, and resources to help you cultivate mindfulness and manage stress.

American Psychological Association's Stress Management resources: Visit the APA website for articles and resources on managing stress and promoting well-being.

Workshops and seminars:

Consider attending workshops, seminars, or conferences focused on stress management, work-life balance, and personal development. Many organizations offer online and in-person events that can help you build skills and knowledge in these areas.

Support groups and communities:

Seek out local support groups or online communities dedicated to work-life balance and stress management. Connecting with others who share your goals and experiences can be a valuable source of encouragement and support.

In conclusion, achieving work-life balance requires setting boundaries, managing stress, and incorporating self-care practices into your daily routine. By prioritizing your personal values, establishing and communicating your boundaries, and implementing effective stress-management techniques, you can create a more balanced, fulfilling life. Remember to periodically reflect on your progress and make adjustments as needed to maintain balance and well-being. Embrace the journey of personal growth and self-discovery as you work toward achieving work-life balance and living a more harmonious, meaningful life.

Nurturing Relationships and Personal Growth

Achieving work-life balance is not solely about managing time and setting boundaries. It also involves nurturing relationships and personal growth. When you invest time and energy in your relationships and personal development, you create a strong foundation for overall well-being, happiness, and success. In this section, we will discuss the importance of cultivating meaningful relationships, embracing personal growth, and maintaining a healthy work-life balance.

Fostering Meaningful Relationships

Relationships play a crucial role in our lives. They provide support, encouragement, and a sense of belonging. Building and maintaining strong relationships is essential for achieving work-life balance and overall happiness.

Prioritize relationships: Just as you allocate time for work and personal tasks, make sure to set aside time for your relationships. Schedule regular dates with your partner, plan family outings, and make time for friends. Ensuring that you give your relationships the attention they deserve will make them stronger and more fulfilling.

Communicate openly and honestly: Good communication is the cornerstone of any healthy relationship. Practice active listening, express your feelings and needs, and encourage your loved ones to do the same. Open and honest communication helps build trust and understanding, strengthening your connections.

Show appreciation and gratitude: Make it a habit to express appreciation for the people in your life. A simple "thank you" or a heartfelt compliment can go a long way in nurturing your relationships.

Be present: In today's fast-paced world, it's easy to be physically present but mentally elsewhere. When you're spending time with loved ones, make an effort to be fully present and engaged. Put away distractions like your phone, and focus on the conversation and the shared experience.

Offer support: Be there for your loved ones during both good times and bad. Offer a listening ear, a shoulder to cry on, or a helping hand when needed. Showing your support strengthens your relationships and creates a sense of reciprocity and trust.

Embracing Personal Growth

Personal growth is a lifelong journey that involves learning, self-discovery, and development. Investing in your personal growth will not only benefit your relationships but also help you achieve a balanced and fulfilling life.

Set personal goals: Take some time to reflect on your values, dreams, and aspirations. Set specific, measurable, attainable, relevant, and time-bound (SMART) goals that align with your values and vision for your life. These goals will serve as a roadmap for your personal growth journey.

Learn from experiences: Embrace every experience, both positive and negative, as an opportunity to learn and grow. Reflect on your experiences, identify the lessons you can take away, and use this newfound knowledge to inform your future actions and decisions.

Engage in continuous learning: Commit to learning something new every day, whether it's through reading, attending workshops, or enrolling in online courses. Continuous learning allows you to expand your knowledge, develop new skills, and stay up-to-date with the latest trends and best practices in your field.

Seek feedback: Regularly seek feedback from your friends, family, and colleagues. Constructive feedback can help you identify areas for improvement and set the stage for growth and development.

Embrace change: Change is an inevitable part of life. Instead of resisting change, learn to embrace it and adapt to new circumstances. This adaptability will serve you well in your personal and professional life and foster resilience in the face of adversity.

Practical Tools and Techniques for Nurturing Relationships and Personal Growth

Journaling: Regularly writing down your thoughts and feelings can help you gain clarity and self-awareness, process emotions, and track your personal growth journey. You can also use journaling to set goals, plan your time, and reflect on your relationships.

Mindfulness meditation

Mindfulness meditation: Practicing mindfulness meditation can help you become more present in your daily life and improve your relationships. By focusing on your breath and observing your thoughts and feelings without judgment, you can cultivate a greater sense of self-awareness, empathy, and emotional regulation.

Time management techniques: Effective time management is essential for maintaining work-life balance and nurturing your relationships. Techniques such as the Pomodoro Technique, time blocking, and the Eisenhower Matrix can help you prioritize tasks and allocate time more efficiently.

Active listening exercises: To improve your communication skills and strengthen your relationships, practice active listening exercises. This involves fully concentrating on the speaker, avoiding interrupting, asking clarifying questions, and summarizing what you've heard to ensure understanding.

Personal development workshops and seminars: Attend workshops, seminars, or conferences that focus on personal growth, communication, or relationship-building. These events provide valuable insights, tools, and techniques to help you improve your interpersonal skills and personal development.

Setting Realistic Expectations and Maintaining Flexibility

Achieving work-life balance and nurturing your relationships and personal growth requires setting realistic expectations and maintaining flexibility. Understand that progress may be slow at times and that setbacks are a natural part of the journey. Be kind to yourself and adjust your expectations as needed.

It's also important to remain flexible and open to change. Life is unpredictable, and circumstances may shift, requiring you to adapt your goals and plans. Embrace these changes and view them as opportunities for growth and learning.

Checkpoints and Reflection

Regularly assess your progress toward achieving work-life balance and personal growth. Set checkpoints or milestones to help you stay on track and evaluate your progress. Reflect on your experiences, successes, and challenges, and use this information to inform your future actions and decisions.

Resources for Further Learning

There are numerous resources available to help you continue your journey toward work-life balance, nurturing relationships, and personal growth. Consider exploring the following:

Books: There are countless books on topics related to work-life balance, relationships, and personal growth. Some popular titles include "The 7 Habits of Highly Effective People" by Stephen Covey, "The 5 Love Languages" by Gary Chapman, and "Mindset: The New Psychology of Success" by Carol S. Dweck.

Online courses: Platforms like Coursera, Udemy, and LinkedIn Learning offer a wide range of courses on personal development, communication, and relationship-building.

Podcasts: Listening to podcasts can be a convenient way to gain valuable insights and inspiration on your personal growth journey. Some popular personal development podcasts include "The Life Coach School Podcast," "The Best One Yet," and "The Tony Robbins Podcast."

Blogs and websites: Many personal development experts and organizations maintain blogs and websites with helpful articles, tips, and resources. Some notable examples include Tiny Buddha, Zen Habits, and The Art of Charm.

In conclusion, achieving work-life balance involves nurturing your relationships and embracing personal growth. By prioritizing your connections, setting realistic expectations, and continuously learning and growing, you can create a fulfilling, well-rounded life. Remember to be patient with yourself and enjoy the journey, for it is through our experiences and connections that we truly find happiness and success.

The Importance of Self-Care and Mindfulness

In today's fast-paced world, achieving work-life balance often seems elusive. The demands of work, family, and personal life can be overwhelming, leaving you feeling stressed and depleted. It's essential to recognize that taking care of yourself is not a luxury; it's a necessity. In this section, we'll delve into the importance of self-care and mindfulness, offering practical tools, techniques, and resources to help you integrate these practices into your daily life.

Caring for Yourself: A Core Principle of Balance

Self-care is the practice of intentionally engaging in activities that promote physical, emotional, and mental well-being. By prioritizing self-care, you create a foundation from which you can more effectively manage stress, cope with challenges, and maintain balance in your life.

Relatable Experiences: The Power of Self-Care

Consider the story of Sarah, a successful marketing executive who consistently put in long hours at work and rarely took time for herself.

Over time, Sarah's health began to suffer, and she realized that she needed to make a change. By incorporating self-care practices into her daily routine, Sarah was able to improve her well-being, increase her productivity, and create a more balanced life.

Understanding Mindfulness: The Key to Presence and Balance

Mindfulness is the practice of cultivating nonjudgmental awareness of the present moment. By embracing mindfulness, you can develop greater self-awareness, reduce stress, and enhance your overall well-being. Mindfulness can be practiced through formal meditation or by incorporating mindful awareness into everyday activities.

Practical Tools and Techniques for Self-Care and Mindfulness

Here are some practical tools and techniques to help you integrate self-care and mindfulness into your daily life:

Establish a daily self-care routine: Dedicate time each day to activities that nourish your body, mind, and spirit. This might include exercise, journaling, meditation, or spending time in nature.

Practice mindful eating: Be present and fully engaged during meals, savoring the taste, texture, and aroma of your food. This can lead to greater satisfaction and help prevent overeating.

Set boundaries with technology: Establish boundaries around your use of technology to prevent it from consuming your life. Consider implementing a digital detox or setting designated times for checking email and social media.

Cultivate a gratitude practice: Each day, take a few moments to reflect on the things for which you're grateful. This simple practice can have a profound impact on your overall well-being and perspective on life.

Engage in regular physical activity: Exercise is essential for maintaining physical and mental health. Find activities you enjoy and aim to incorporate at least 30 minutes of moderate-intensity exercise most days of the week.

Realistic Expectations and Flexibility

When integrating self-care and mindfulness practices into your life, it's essential to set realistic expectations and maintain flexibility. Understand that progress may be slow and that setbacks are a natural part of the journey. Be patient with yourself and adjust your expectations and practices as needed.

Creating Checkpoints and Reflection Opportunities

Regularly assess your progress in integrating self-care and mindfulness practices into your life. Set checkpoints or milestones to help you stay on track and evaluate your progress. Reflect on your experiences, successes, and challenges, and use this information to inform your future actions and decisions.

Resources for Further Learning

There are numerous resources available to help you continue your journey toward self-care and mindfulness. Consider exploring the following:

Books: There are countless books on topics related to self-care and mindfulness. Some popular titles include "The Miracle of Mindfulness" by Thich Nhat Hanh, "The Self-Care Solution" by Jennifer Ashton, MD, and "Self-Care for the Real World" by Nadra Narain and Katia Narain Phillips.

Online courses: Several reputable websites offer online courses in self-care and mindfulness, such as Coursera, Udemy, and Insight Timer. These courses typically feature expert instruction and guided exercises to help you develop and refine your self-care and mindfulness practices.

Podcasts: Podcasts can be a great way to learn about self-care and mindfulness on the go. Some popular options include "The One You Feed," "The Mindful Kind," and "The Self-Care Chronicles."

Apps: Numerous apps are designed to support self-care and mindfulness practices. Some popular options include Headspace, Calm, and Insight Timer, which offer guided meditations, mindfulness exercises, and relaxation techniques.

Workshops and retreats: Participating in workshops or retreats focused on self-care and mindfulness can be a transformative experience. These immersive events provide the opportunity to learn from experts, connect with like-minded individuals, and deepen your practice.

Questions and Answers to Enhance Your Journey

As you embark on your journey toward greater self-care and mindfulness, you may have questions or encounter challenges. Here are some common questions and answers to help you navigate your path:

How do I find time for self-care in my busy schedule?

To make self-care a priority, consider scheduling dedicated time for self-care activities in your calendar, just as you would for any other important commitment. Also, look for opportunities to integrate self-care practices into your existing routine, such as taking a walk during your lunch break or practicing mindful breathing during your daily commute.

What if I struggle with maintaining a consistent mindfulness practice?

Consistency is essential for reaping the benefits of mindfulness. If you struggle with maintaining a regular practice, try setting aside a specific time each day for mindfulness exercises or meditation, such as first thing in the morning or right before bed. Additionally, consider using guided meditation resources or attending group meditation sessions to help you stay accountable and committed to your practice.

How do I know if my self-care and mindfulness practices are working?

The impact of self-care and mindfulness practices may be subtle and gradual, making it challenging to determine their effectiveness. Some potential indicators of progress include increased self-awareness, reduced stress, improved emotional regulation, enhanced relationships, and a greater sense of overall well-being. Remember that progress may be slow, and setbacks are a natural part of the journey. Be patient with yourself and adjust your expectations and practices as needed.

In conclusion, the pursuit of work-life balance is a continuous journey that requires intentionality, self-awareness, and dedication. By integrating self-care and mindfulness practices into your daily life, you can create a foundation for greater balance, resilience, and overall well-being. As you embark on this journey, remember to set realistic expectations, maintain flexibility, and leverage the wealth of resources available to support you in your personal growth and development.

Chapter Ten

Chapter 10: The Path to Lasting Success

Embracing Lifelong Learning

In today's ever-evolving world, the key to achieving lasting success lies in our ability to continuously learn, adapt, and grow. By embracing lifelong learning, we not only enhance our skills and knowledge but also cultivate a growth mindset that enables us to overcome challenges and seize opportunities. This section will delve into the importance of lifelong learning, provide actionable advice for integrating learning into your daily life, and offer resources to support your personal and professional growth.

The Importance of Lifelong Learning in a Dynamic World

The world is constantly changing, with technological advancements and shifts in the global economy disrupting traditional industries and career paths. To remain competitive and relevant, it is crucial to stay informed and continuously develop new skills and knowledge. Lifelong learning is not just about acquiring new information but also about developing the ability to think critically, problem-solve, and adapt to new situations. By embracing lifelong learning, we can:

Stay competitive in the job market: As industries evolve, the skills and knowledge required for success also change. Staying up to date with the latest trends, technologies, and best practices can help you maintain your employability and advance in your career.

Foster personal growth: Lifelong learning enables us to cultivate new interests, deepen our understanding of the world, and enhance our overall quality of life.

Develop resilience: Learning how to navigate change and adapt to new circumstances is a vital skill for personal and professional success. By embracing lifelong learning, we cultivate the ability to bounce back from setbacks and face challenges with confidence.

Improve decision-making and problem-solving abilities: By continually expanding our knowledge and honing our critical thinking skills, we can make better-informed decisions and develop creative solutions to complex problems.

Build a network of connections: Engaging in learning opportunities, such as conferences, workshops, or online courses, can help you connect with like-minded individuals and expand your professional network.

Strategies for Integrating Lifelong Learning into Your Daily Life

To truly embrace lifelong learning, it is essential to make it an integral part of your daily routine. Here are some practical strategies to help you incorporate learning into your life:

Set clear learning goals: Identify specific areas in which you would like to expand your knowledge or skills, and set clear, achievable goals to guide your learning journey. By defining your objectives, you can maintain focus and motivation as you work towards personal and professional growth.

Allocate dedicated time for learning: Schedule regular time in your calendar for learning activities, such as reading, online courses, or attending workshops. Treat these commitments as you would any other important appointment to ensure that learning remains a priority.

Embrace diverse learning opportunities: Lifelong learning can take many forms, including formal education, self-directed study, experiential learning, and mentorship. Be open to exploring different learning avenues and choose methods that align with your goals and preferred learning style.

Cultivate a growth mindset: Embrace the belief that your abilities and intelligence can be developed through dedication and hard work. A growth mindset can help you overcome obstacles, learn from failure, and maintain motivation throughout your learning journey.

Share your knowledge and experiences: Teaching others can be a powerful way to reinforce your learning and deepen your understanding of a subject. Look for opportunities to share your insights and experiences, such as presenting at conferences, writing articles or blog posts, or mentoring others in your field.

Resources for Supporting Your Lifelong Learning Journey

To support your lifelong learning journey, consider leveraging the following resources:

Online courses: Platforms such as Coursera, edX, and Udemy offer a wide range of online courses in various subjects, allowing you to expand your knowledge and skills at your own pace and on your

own schedule. Many courses are taught by experts in their respective fields and offer valuable insights, practical exercises, and opportunities for interaction with other learners.

Books and articles: Reading books, articles, and research papers can help deepen your understanding of a subject and expose you to new ideas and perspectives. Consider setting a reading goal, such as a certain number of books per month, to maintain a consistent learning habit.

Podcasts and webinars: Listening to podcasts and attending webinars can provide valuable insights and inspiration from experts in various fields. These resources can be easily integrated into your daily routine, such as during your commute or while exercising.

Professional associations and networking groups: Joining industry-specific associations and networking groups can help you stay informed about the latest trends, connect with like-minded professionals, and access resources such as workshops, conferences, and publications.

Mentors and coaches: Seeking guidance from mentors or coaches can provide personalized support and insights to help you navigate your learning journey and overcome challenges. Look for individuals who have experience in your field of interest and are willing to share their knowledge and expertise.

Volunteer opportunities and internships: Engaging in hands-on learning experiences, such as volunteering or internships, can help you develop new skills, gain practical experience, and build connections in your industry.

By embracing lifelong learning and making it an integral part of your daily life, you can achieve lasting personal and professional success. Remember to set clear learning goals, allocate dedicated time for learning, explore diverse learning opportunities, cultivate a growth mindset, and leverage available resources to support your journey. With dedication, persistence, and a passion for growth, you will be well-equipped to navigate the ever-evolving landscape of today's dynamic world and forge a fulfilling and successful path.

The Power of Persistence and Patience

The journey to lasting success is often filled with challenges, setbacks, and obstacles that test your resilience and determination. The ability to persist in the face of adversity and exhibit patience in your pursuit of success is an essential quality shared by many accomplished individuals. In this section, we will explore the power of persistence and patience, offering insights and guidance to help you cultivate these qualities in your own life.

Drawing from Real-Life Experiences: Stories of Persistence and Patience

Throughout history, countless individuals have demonstrated the power of persistence and patience in achieving their goals. These stories offer valuable lessons and inspiration for your own journey:

Thomas Edison: Edison's invention of the light bulb was the result of thousands of failed experiments. His unwavering persistence and patience eventually led to the creation of a functional light bulb and revolutionized modern life.

J.K. Rowling: Before the success of the Harry Potter series, Rowling faced numerous rejections from publishers and struggled with personal challenges. Her persistence and patience eventually paid off, leading to the phenomenal success of the series and her status as one of the most successful authors of all time.

Oprah Winfrey: Winfrey's rise to fame was not without its challenges, including overcoming poverty, abuse, and discrimination. Her persistence, patience, and determination enabled her to become one of the most influential media personalities and philanthropists in the world.

The Science Behind Persistence and Patience

Research has shown that persistence and patience are closely linked to success in various aspects of life, including personal and professional endeavors. Key findings include:

Grit: Psychologist Angela Duckworth's research on "grit" – the combination of passion and perseverance – has demonstrated that this quality is a significant predictor of success. Gritty individuals are more likely to achieve their goals, overcome setbacks, and maintain their motivation in the face of challenges.

Delayed gratification: Studies on delayed gratification have shown that individuals who can resist immediate rewards in favor of long-term gains tend to exhibit greater success in various aspects of life, including education, career, and personal relationships. Cultivating patience and the ability to delay gratification can improve your chances of achieving lasting success.

Taking Action: Cultivating Persistence and Patience in Your Life

To develop persistence and patience in your own life, consider the following strategies and techniques:

Set clear, realistic goals: Establish specific, achievable objectives that align with your values and aspirations. Breaking down larger goals into smaller, manageable steps can help you maintain your motivation and focus.

Embrace a growth mindset: Adopting a growth mindset – the belief that abilities and intelligence can be developed through effort, learning, and persistence – can improve your resilience and determination in the face of challenges.

Develop a strong support network: Surround yourself with individuals who encourage and support your goals. A strong support network can provide invaluable encouragement and guidance, helping you stay motivated and persevere through tough times.

Manage your expectations: Recognize that setbacks and obstacles are a natural part of the journey to success. Adopting a realistic perspective can help you maintain your patience and persistence in the face of adversity.

Reflect on your progress: Regularly reviewing your progress and acknowledging your achievements can help you maintain your motivation and persistence. Celebrate your successes, learn from your setbacks, and adjust your strategies as needed.

Cultivate self-compassion: Practicing self-compassion – being kind and understanding toward yourself, especially when facing setbacks or challenges – can help you maintain your patience and persistence in the face of adversity.

Develop coping strategies: Learn to manage stress and maintain a healthy balance between work and personal life. Techniques such as meditation, mindfulness, and regular exercise can help you cope with stress, enhance your resilience, and support your overall well-being.

Visualize success: Regularly envisioning yourself achieving your goals can help maintain your motivation and persistence. Visualization techniques have been used by many successful individuals to help them stay focused on their objectives and maintain a positive mindset.

Learn from failure: Embrace setbacks and failures as opportunities for growth and learning. Analyze your mistakes, identify areas for improvement, and use this knowledge to refine your strategies and increase your chances of success.

Checkpoints and Reflection: Assessing Your Persistence and Patience

Periodically assess your progress and evaluate your level of persistence and patience. Reflect on the following questions:

How have you demonstrated persistence and patience in your pursuit of your goals? Can you recall specific instances where these qualities have helped you overcome challenges or setbacks?

Are there areas in your life where you could improve your persistence and patience? What strategies or techniques could you implement to cultivate these qualities further?

How has your support network contributed to your persistence and patience? Are there specific individuals who have played a significant role in encouraging and supporting you in your journey?

Resources for Further Learning

To deepen your understanding of persistence and patience and develop these qualities in your own life, consider the following resources:

Books:

"Grit: The Power of Passion and Perseverance" by Angela Duckworth

"The Power of Patience: How to Slow the Rush and Enjoy More Happiness, Success, and Peace of Mind Every Day" by M.J. Ryan

"Mindset: The New Psychology of Success" by Carol S. Dweck

TED Talks:

Angela Duckworth: "Grit: The Power of Passion and Perseverance"

Carol Dweck: "The Power of Believing That You Can Improve"

Eduardo Briceño: "How to Get Better at the Things You Care About"

Online courses:

"Learning How to Learn: Powerful Mental Tools to Help You Master Tough Subjects" (Coursera)

"Developing Grit, Resilience, and a Growth Mindset" (LinkedIn Learning)

In conclusion, persistence and patience are essential qualities in the pursuit of lasting success. By embracing lifelong learning, developing a growth mindset, and cultivating resilience, you can strengthen these qualities and increase your chances of achieving your goals. Reflect on your progress, learn from your setbacks, and celebrate your successes as you continue on your journey toward lasting success.

Celebrating Success and Staying Humble

Success is not a destination; it's a journey filled with small wins, lessons, and growth opportunities. Celebrating your achievements is crucial for maintaining motivation, but staying humble and grounded is equally essential to ensure lasting success. In this section, we will explore the importance of appreciating your accomplishments while maintaining a humble attitude, and provide practical strategies to help you strike the right balance.

Recognizing Your Achievements

Taking the time to acknowledge and celebrate your accomplishments is vital for maintaining a positive mindset and fostering personal growth. Consider the following suggestions to help you recognize your achievements:

Reflect on your progress: Regularly review your goals and the progress you've made toward achieving them. Make a list of the milestones you've reached and the obstacles you've overcome to gain a clear understanding of how far you've come.

Share your successes: Sharing your achievements with friends, family, or colleagues can help reinforce your progress and boost your motivation. Don't hesitate to share your wins on social media or within your professional network, as this can lead to opportunities for further growth and development.

Reward yourself: Establish a system of rewards for when you reach specific milestones or complete challenging tasks. These rewards can be as simple as treating yourself to a favorite meal, taking a day off, or indulging in a hobby you enjoy.

Express gratitude: Cultivate a habit of expressing gratitude for the people, opportunities, and experiences that have contributed to your achievements. This practice not only promotes a positive mindset but also helps you maintain a sense of humility and perspective.

Maintaining Humility: The Key to Lasting Success

While it's essential to celebrate your accomplishments, maintaining a humble attitude is equally important for achieving lasting success. Here are some strategies to help you stay grounded and humble:

Embrace a growth mindset: Adopt a mindset that values continuous learning and personal development. Understand that success is an ongoing journey, and there will always be more to learn, new challenges to face, and room for growth.

Seek feedback: Regularly solicit feedback from others, both in your personal and professional life, to gain valuable insights into your strengths and areas for improvement. Be open to constructive criticism and use it as an opportunity for growth.

Surround yourself with diverse perspectives: Engage with individuals who have different experiences, backgrounds, and skill sets to broaden your horizons and challenge your assumptions. This exposure can help you stay grounded and open to new ideas.

Practice humility in your interactions: In your interactions with others, be respectful, empathetic, and considerate. Recognize the value that each person brings to the table and be willing to learn from their experiences and perspectives.

Cultivating Balance: Celebrating Success and Staying Humble

To strike a balance between celebrating your achievements and maintaining humility, consider the following strategies:

Set realistic expectations: Set achievable goals and expectations for yourself, while understanding that setbacks and obstacles are a natural part of the journey. This approach will help you maintain perspective and stay grounded in the face of both success and adversity.

Keep a journal: Maintain a journal to document your accomplishments, lessons learned, and areas for growth. This practice can help you develop self-awareness and maintain a balanced perspective on your journey to success.

Engage in regular self-reflection: Set aside time for introspection and self-assessment. Reflect on your actions, decisions, and progress, and consider how you can continue to grow and improve moving forward.

Be a mentor: Share your knowledge and experience with others by becoming a mentor or coach. This act of service can help you maintain a sense of humility and perspective while also providing valuable support to those who are just starting their journey to success.

Celebrate others' successes: Actively recognize and celebrate the accomplishments of those around you. Supporting others in their journey not only fosters a positive environment but also helps you maintain a humble attitude and a sense of perspective.

Focus on your core values: Identify your core values and let them guide your decisions and actions. By staying true to your values, you can maintain a sense of integrity and humility throughout your journey to success.

Resources for Further Learning

To support your growth and maintain a balance between celebrating success and staying humble, consider exploring the following resources:

Books:

"Mindset: The New Psychology of Success" by Carol S. Dweck

"The Power of Now: A Guide to Spiritual Enlightenment" by Eckhart Tolle

"The Gifts of Imperfection: Let Go of Who You Think You're Supposed to Be and Embrace Who You Are" by Brené Brown

Websites and online resources:

TED Talks (www.ted.com): Explore a vast library of inspiring talks on a wide range of topics related to personal growth, success, and humility.

Harvard Business Review (www.hbr.org): Access insightful articles and research on leadership, personal development, and success.

The Greater Good Science Center at UC Berkeley (www.greatergood.berkeley.edu): Discover research-based resources on topics such as gratitude, humility, and happiness.

Workshops and courses:

Local community centers, universities, and professional organizations often offer workshops, seminars, and courses on personal development, leadership, and success. These opportunities can help you further your growth and maintain a balanced perspective on your journey.

In conclusion, achieving lasting success requires a delicate balance between celebrating your achievements and maintaining a humble attitude. By implementing the strategies and resources discussed in this section, you can continue to grow personally and professionally while staying grounded and true to your values. Remember that success is an ongoing journey, and by embracing lifelong learning, persistence, and humility, you can create a meaningful and fulfilling life.

Passing the Torch: Inspiring the Next Generation

As you continue on your journey toward lasting success, it's essential to remember that you're not just building a better life for yourself but also creating a positive impact on the world around you. One of the most powerful ways to leave a lasting legacy is by inspiring and mentoring the next generation. By sharing your knowledge, experiences, and wisdom, you can help others achieve their goals and reach their full potential. In this section, we'll explore the importance of passing the torch to the next generation and offer practical advice on how you can inspire and empower others.

The Ripple Effect: Why Inspiring the Next Generation Matters

When you invest in the growth and development of others, you create a ripple effect that can extend far beyond your immediate sphere of influence. By nurturing the talents and dreams of the next generation, you're not only helping them succeed but also contributing to the betterment of society as a whole. Consider the following benefits of inspiring the next generation:

Creating a positive impact: By sharing your knowledge and experience, you can help others avoid common pitfalls and accelerate their progress toward their goals. This, in turn, increases the likelihood that they'll make a positive impact in their own lives and the lives of others.

Building a legacy: As you inspire and empower others, you create a living legacy that will continue to impact the world long after you're gone. By investing in the next generation, you're ensuring that your values, wisdom, and insights will continue to shape the future.

Personal growth: Mentoring and inspiring others can also lead to personal growth and self-discovery. As you teach and guide others, you'll deepen your understanding of yourself and your own journey, further enhancing your ability to achieve lasting success.

Guiding Lights: Strategies for Inspiring the Next Generation

Now that you understand the importance of inspiring the next generation, let's explore some practical strategies for doing so:

Share your story: One of the most powerful ways to inspire others is by sharing your own personal journey. Be open and honest about your successes, challenges, and lessons learned, and don't be afraid to show vulnerability. Your story can serve as a roadmap for others to follow, giving them the courage to pursue their own dreams.

Be a mentor: Mentoring is a powerful way to support and guide others in their personal and professional development. Seek out opportunities to mentor individuals within your industry, community, or social circles, and commit to providing ongoing guidance, encouragement, and support.

Teach and educate: Share your knowledge and expertise by teaching workshops, hosting seminars, or offering educational resources, such as articles, podcasts, or videos. By sharing your wisdom, you can help others acquire the skills and knowledge they need to succeed.

Lead by example: Demonstrate the qualities you wish to instill in others through your own actions and behavior. Embody the values of integrity, perseverance, and resilience, and model the habits and mindset that have led to your success.

Offer encouragement and support: Be a source of support and encouragement for others as they pursue their goals. Celebrate their achievements, offer constructive feedback, and help them navigate setbacks and challenges.

Build a supportive community: Create spaces where individuals can come together to learn, grow, and support one another. This can be done through workshops, mastermind groups, or online forums, where people can share their experiences, insights, and resources.

Reflecting on Your Impact

As you work to inspire the next generation, it's essential to periodically reflect on your impact and consider the following questions:

How have you been a positive influence on others? What specific actions have you taken to empower and inspire those around you?

What progress have you seen in the individuals you've mentored or supported? How have their lives changed as a result of your guidance?

How has your own personal growth and self-awareness been influenced by your efforts to inspire others?

What new insights or lessons have you learned through your interactions with the next generation?

By reflecting on these questions, you can gain a deeper understanding of the impact you're making and identify areas where you can further enhance your efforts.

Providing Resources for Continued Growth

To help the next generation reach their full potential, it's important to provide them with access to resources that can support their ongoing growth and development. Consider the following options:

Recommend books, articles, podcasts, or videos that have had a significant impact on your own journey and can provide valuable insights for others.

Connect individuals with industry experts or thought leaders who can offer specialized knowledge and guidance.

Share information about workshops, conferences, or seminars that can help expand their knowledge and skills.

Encourage them to join professional organizations, networking groups, or online forums where they can connect with others who share similar goals and interests.

By providing these resources, you're equipping the next generation with the tools they need to continue growing, learning, and achieving success.

In Conclusion

Passing the torch to the next generation is a vital component of achieving lasting success. By inspiring and mentoring others, you're creating a ripple effect that can have a profound impact on the world around you. Embrace the responsibility of being a guiding light and dedicate yourself to empowering the next generation to achieve their dreams. In doing so, you'll leave a lasting legacy that will continue to inspire and shape the future for generations to come.

Epilogue

As we close this book, remember that the journey doesn't end here. It's a never-ending pursuit of learning, growth, resilience, and unyielding determination. Embrace the chaos, the challenge, the uncertainty. Because no one ever said it would be easy, but I promise you, it'll be worth it.

"Dreams don't work unless you do." - John C. Maxwell

Acknowledgements

Gratitude to everyone who has been part of this journey. From the dreamers who dared to share their stories, to the readers like you who embraced them.

About the Author

The author, an acclaimed life coach, business consultant, and motivational speaker, has spent decades guiding individuals and organizations toward success. Born into humble beginnings, their personal journey of grit and resilience has been as inspirational as the countless success stories they have helped shape.

The author holds several advanced degrees and certifications in business and personal development, but it is their real-world experience - the trials, errors, successes, and hard-won wisdom - that truly distinguishes them.

With a refreshing blend of frankness and empathy, the author challenges, inspires, and guides readers and clients alike. Through personal anecdotes, well-researched insights, and a no-nonsense approach, they have a unique way of turning complex challenges into actionable strategies.

In addition to "Who the F*ck Told You It Would Be Easy?", the author has penned several best-selling books on personal growth, entrepreneurship, and leadership. When not writing or coaching, they can be found leading workshops worldwide or spending quality time with family and a cherished golden retriever.

The author's journey is a testament to the message they share - that while the path to success may not be easy, it's always worth the struggle. The author lives the truth of their work every day, proving that with persistence, patience, and a bit of grit, anyone can redefine their boundaries and achieve what they once thought was impossible.

www.ingramcontent.com/pod-product-compliance
Lightning Source LLC
Chambersburg PA
CBHW071237070526
44583CB00017B/2216